Micro to Mainframe

MICRO TO MAINFRAME
Creating an Integrated Environment

Michael Durr and Dwayne Walker

ADDISON-WESLEY PUBLISHING COMPANY, INC.
Reading, Massachusetts • Menlo Park, California •
Don Mills, Ontario • Wokingham, England •
Amsterdam • Sydney • Singapore • Toyko • Mexico
City • Bogotá • Santiago • San Juan

Library of Congress Cataloging-in-Publication Data

Durr, Michael.
  Micro to mainframe.

  Includes index.
  1. Microcomputers.   2. Electronic data processing—Distributed processing.   3. Computer networks.   I. Walker, Dwayne.   II. Title.
  QA76.5.D76   1985   004.6   85-15054
  ISBN 0–201–11155–1

Text design by Joyce C. Weston

Cover design by Marshall Henrichs

ABCDEFGHIJK-HA-898765

CONTENTS

ILLUSTRATIONS

INTRODUCTION

SOME people portray the micro-mainframe relationship as an irresistible force meeting an immovable object. The description evokes images of an army of antlike microcomputers attacking the fortresses of data processing in a fight to the finish.

The lines are certainly not that clearly drawn, but a confrontational situation does exist. Its cause is found in the fundamental differences between the micro user and the DP professional. Micro users are often highly trained business professionals with little knowledge of computing practices. The only thing that micro users want to know is how to get to the data so that they can do their jobs.

At the same time, the mainframe DP department is staffed with computing professionals. Their jobs are organizing and protecting data and making that data available to users through a network of easily controlled dumb terminals.

Because of this dichotomy of purposes and backgrounds people frequently don't understand the issues and implications of their actions in an integrated micro-mainframe environment.

Technical and management issues are both critical to successful micro-mainframe integration. For micro-mainframe integration to work, however, a certain amount of compromising and understanding is required from both the micro and the mainframe areas. They can no longer work as two independent environments.

When micro users are linked into the mainframe system, they usually find themselves saddled with an inconvenient assortment of new rules and procedures. They are told what data they can store and what data they can access, what applications software they can use, and how much data they can move in a single transfer. They are given log-in names and passwords and lectures on data integrity.

In essence, the "personal" microcomputer users become part of a community of users. Membership in this new community offers access to highly useful data and computing resources not available to the user of a stand-alone micro. It also carries additional responsibilities. One of the purposes of this book is to explain the micro-mainframe environment to users. The book explains the new capabilities that the mainframe connection brings to the micro user and the reasons behind the new responsibilities.

From the data processing manager's point of view, micro-mainframe integration presents a different set of issues. The first issue is largely mechanical — can micros be integrated into a mainframe system? Managers quickly learn not only that the link is possible but also that it's possible using a variety of different methods. Each of these methods carries its own benefits and costs, which must be evaluated.

The next issue that managers must address is resource management. The microcomputer can place a heavy strain on computing resources, especially the mainframe CPU time and the communications network. Unmanaged, the micro has the potential of bringing the entire computing system to a standstill.

The microcomputer can also strain the computing budget. Unit costs of microcomputers are relatively low, enabling many departments to buy them with operational funds. Yet, although the unit costs are low, the overall workstation costs for both hardware and software may be significantly higher than the cost of alternative computing solutions. As a result, the capital outlay for computing in some organizations has tripled since the premicro era.

Management needs a plan that encompasses the technical and

managerial issues of micro-mainframe integration. This book is designed to provide the basic information necessary for the development of that plan.

The authors wish to thank the many people who helped in the preparation of this material. Among these are our friends and colleagues in the Information Center Management Association (Los Angeles) and the Personal Computer Professional Association (Los Angeles). Corporate members of these groups freely share information and experiences with other members. We've often seen the results of months of study in micro-mainframe integration presented in a single meeting and disseminated to all members. We highly recommend participation in such groups as a way to maintain expertise in micro-mainframe integration.

Many people supported us with a combination of input and forebearance that we greatly appreciated: the data processing instructors of Cerritos College (California) and California State University, Fullerton; Marvin Brown, Arthur Walker, Elnora Walker, Derrick Walker, and Darrell Walker.

1. Mainframe-to-Micro: The Potential

IN many ways, the microcomputer is the ideal workstation. It's inexpensive, easy to use, and productive. Most importantly, people like micros.

The mainframe computer, on the other hand, is the ideal data-storage system. The mainframe's ability to manage huge amounts of data and coordinate diverse activities is unmatched.

Several years ago, when we started hearing that the micro-computer would be used as a mainframe terminal, it didn't come as a big surprise. There was a problem, however; no practical way existed to link the two technologies at that time. Today, the mechanical problem of linkage has largely disappeared, because many products have been offered to bridge the gap between mainframe and micro. Although all of these products can be described as mainframe-micro links, their costs, features, and impacts differ radically, creating a new problem for data processing managers. That problem is how to select the best mainframe-micro link.

An even greater problem is that once the link has been established, a whole new group of people will have access to the mainframe. More importantly, they will have access through a microcomputer, a machine with far more independent power than any previous workstation. The challenge is to give these people the support they need while protecting corporate data from potentially devastating misuse.

To see how the mainframe-micro link can work, consider the following typical implementation. Any terms in the example that are new to you will be explained as they're discussed in subsequent chapters.

THE XYZ CORPORATION

The XYZ Corporation is a service-oriented organization with a heavy investment in computing and data processing. Its DP department manages storage and acquisition of data through an extensive network of mainframe computers and terminals. DP's responsibility includes supporting users of this data in every department and remote site within the corporation.

Last year the corporation commissioned a thorough analysis of its data processing services. The study revealed significant problems: lack of responsiveness to users' needs; resistance to distributed computing; complex software running on the mainframe; poor performance of a data communications network; users are vulnerable to mainframe downtime; and a three-year backlog in programming. As a result of the study, the corporation instituted a major reorganization of its computing services.

REORGANIZATION OF DP SERVICES

The new structure is designed to fully integrate DP computing resources for maximum utility and information availability. The mainframe computer now has a direct host-to-terminal network with 3270 terminals, asynchronous terminals, and terminal-emulating microcomputers. A time-sharing system, also based on the mainframe, gives users access to mainframe hardware through a similar blend of terminals and terminal-emulating micros.

Most departments at XYZ now have DP networks of their own, with terminals and micros connected to departmental minicomputers. Local area networks (LANs) interconnect microcomputers and allow personnel to communicate and share information and peripherals. Workstations (terminals and microcomputers that are connected to the minicomputers) and

LANs can communicate with the mainframe. These communications can be interactive (immediate processing) or batch (scheduled processing).

From a typical microcomputer workstation, a person can download data from the central database and use that information as the basis for reports, spreadsheet analyses, and graphics. This retrieved data can be stored at the workstation, at the shared departmental storage system, or at the mainframe computer. Users have the option of reserving their data for personal use or making it accessible to others on the network.

An additional advantage of the new system is the wide range of information available to users through the network-attached microcomputer. This includes a library of software applications, newsletters, and training and applications tips for micro users. Information remains on-line continually and can be accessed at times when an analyst or other support personnel may not be available.

The XYZ Corporation has thus implemented a fully distributed computing network (see figure 1–1). A key component of the company's strategy is the integration of the microcomputer and its user into the system. Management believes that bringing computing resources and support closer to the end-user will help the corporation meet its data processing needs more efficiently.

THE INTRODUCTION OF THE MICROCOMPUTER

The problems uncovered by the XYZ Corporation are common in today's corporate data processing. Businesses are increasingly data-driven, a situation that places insatiable demands on DP departments and creates extensive backlogs of work. Rather than increase the size of the DP department, the solution seems to be found in giving end-users more control over their own data. The microcomputer offers a means to that end (see figure 1–2).

The popularity of the microcomputer is not based primarily on high performance or cost-effectiveness. Indeed, many alternative solutions offer better performance at better prices. The appeal of the micro is that it frees the end-user from dependence upon DP departments and offers the potential for increased productivity. The relatively low cost of the microcomputer and the

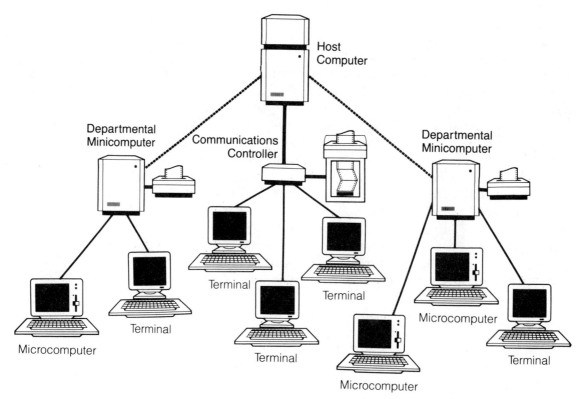

ready availability of good micro application software allows a person to do a job on a micro, without having to ask DP to write special programs.

    The micro's functional capabilities are not its only attributes. Microcomputers have brought computing to people who in some cases have not used any type of automated office tool before. The general enthusiasm for the microcomputer on the part of newcomers to computing improves the micro's potential to increase white-collar productivity.

FIGURE I–I: *XYZ Corporation was able to meet the needs of its end users by implementing a distributed computer communications network that focuses on bringing computer resources closer to the end user.*

FROM STAND-ALONE TO NETWORKED

The role of the microcomputer is continually evolving. Initially, microcomputers were used as "personal productivity tools," a

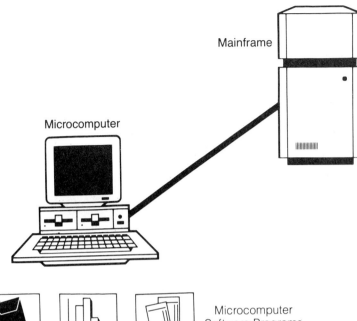

FIGURE 1–2: *The microcomputer offers the benefits of local processing, user-friendly software, and full end-user control.*

Mainframe

Microcomputer

Microcomputer
Software Programs

replacement for pencil, paper, and calculator. Today, however, with sophisticated software available, the micro is able to handle processing that once required a mainframe or minicomputer.

Beyond its stand-alone processing capabilities, the microcomputer has another important capability: it can communicate. This capability is implemented by tying the micro into a communications network, which then connects it to another computer.

One potential drawback of the stand-alone micro is duplication of work, especially when data must be rekeyed. A networked microcomputer can provide an ideal solution to this problem. Virtually all data of significance to a corporation is stored on a central computer. For the data to be used on a micro, it often must be rekeyed manually; but rekeying is time-consuming and may introduce serious errors. Furthermore, with microcomputers isolated from the main system, a discontinuity of information often results. That is, micro users may base their analyses and processing upon seriously outdated information. A microcomputer with a connection to a central computer (host) allows data to be transferred from the mainframe storage area directly to the microcomputer, without rekeying. With little effort, people can quickly update their data.

From a cost standpoint, stand-alone microcomputers can be an expensive, though effective, way to solve a problem. In addition to the basic device, the stand-alone micro is often equipped with a dot matrix printer, a hard disk, and various application software packages. A letter-quality printer, a plotter, and data-backup devices may also be required, depending on the particular workstation. These special devices no doubt create a powerful workstation, but the cost may exceed the potential benefit.

The networked microcomputer reduces the cost of intelligent workstations by permitting the sharing of peripheral devices. For example, instead of buying a letter-quality printer for every micro workstation that might need it, a single letter-quality printer can be purchased and shared by several workstations. Through sharing, an office can justify higher quality peripherals, and a greater variety of them.

INTRODUCTION TO THE MAINFRAME

Microcomputers are most often linked into the mainframe through a time-sharing system. *Time sharing,* or *end-user computing,* is the sharing of a host computer, hence the name *time-sharing.* Through a mainframe-micro link, a micro user can tap into the mainframe system and its processing power. The time-sharing concept, thus, is an extension of the stand-alone system.

Time-sharing, in itself, may not include any processing other than what is needed to make the mainframe's resources useful. The micro is made to emulate a terminal to access the time-sharing system and can also revert to stand-alone mode for processing of data. Simple file transfers can be supported in a time-sharing system; data on a mainframe can be moved down to the micro and back to the mainframe. However, time-sharing does not integrate the micro into production computing. Instead, time-sharing serves as a middle ground, or buffer, between production systems and microcomputers or terminals.

Besides time-sharing, another potential use of micros is in production computing. Production computing involves actual manipulation of mainframe applications, such as payroll, accounts payable, and sales forecasting. Serious consideration should be given to the problem of data sensitivity before micros are integrated with a mainframe in a production environment.

THE MAINFRAME-MICRO LINK

The mainframe computer is used for consolidating, storing, and processing large amounts of data. The microcomputer offers users the ability to analyze and manipulate that data without the need for the DP department. To give micro users access to the mainframe's data, it is necessary to create a link between the mainframe and the microcomputer.

A mainframe cannot be linked to a micro in a single step. Instead, the link is made up of a series of interrelated processes that move data along and eventually make mainframe data usable at the microcomputer. These processes are shown in figure 1–3.

The first step in a linking process is usually a request that is sent from the microcomputer to the mainframe: for example, "Send me the sales figures for the third quarter." The request is created using special link software that can communicate with both the micro and the mainframe environments.

The request goes through the telecommunications system into the mainframe environment. There it contacts the applications product (usually database management software) and begins the process of extracting and downloading; that is, retrieving mainframe data and sending it down to the micro. The requested data is extracted from the mainframe database and a report file is created. Often a request asks the report to be formatted and summarized (numbers totaled and displayed) in a particular way. All this is done at the mainframe in preparation for transmitting the file.

The report may also be translated at the mainframe. In most instances, mainframe data is encoded and stored in different for-

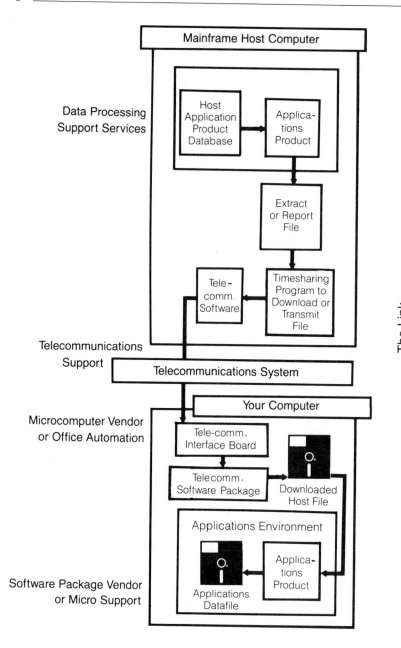

FIGURE I–3: *Data must pass through several steps to go between the mainframe and micro environments. These steps are handled by host applications software, telecommunications, and micro applications software.*

mats from those used at the microcomputer. A translation routine must convert the report to the proper microcomputer format. The report is usually stored on disk or printed at the microcomputer. From the micro disk, the data in the report may be taken by a micro applications package and processed further.

There are many variations to this general mainframe-micro link process. Although all links attempt to make some type of connection between the mainframe and micro, they may follow different paths. The strategy that's eventually selected, along with the way in which it's implemented, will determine the effectiveness of the mainframe-micro link.

PLAN FOR INTEGRATION

In selecting mainframe-micro strategy, managers must develop a detailed plan. Some of the potential problem areas to be considered are functionality, security, cost effectiveness, and integration.

Functionality

Organizations must decide what functions are to be performed at the micro level and what functions will continue to be performed at the mainframe. Determination of tasks performed at each workstation is a vital step in planning a system. What work do you want accomplished at the workstation?

The stand-alone microcomputer can perform a rich variety of functions: word processing, database management, financial modeling, and communications. (The topic of micro capabilities is covered in detail in chapter 2.) The micro can be adapted to emulate nearly any class of terminal in a mainframe environment. Emulation products are available to let micros communicate with most minicomputers and mainframes.

Once the potential capabilities of the micro workstation are understood, the next task is to compare them to the needs of the particular workstation. One brand of micro may not be the answer to all of your requirements. It's also possible that an interface between a micro and your mainframe or mini may not be available.

Security

Protecting the data, which includes controlling access to data for security reasons and protecting the integrity of that data, is made much more difficult in a distributed computing environment. As long as all processing and applications software is centrally located at the mainframe, security can be a relatively simple matter. In a distributed processing environment, however, some computing services may be separated from the central facility and managed locally in departments or remote sites. When local processing and storage must be linked to central processing and storage, new methods must be developed to protect the data.

For years many companies have operated around the premise of a central data processing department. To provide physical security, for example, an organization with a mainframe computer will typically have the machine locked away and will carefully restrict access. This type of physical security is much easier to administer than monitoring the use of hundreds of microcomputers throughout a company.

As workstations proliferate throughout companies, the physical security of computing resources becomes a large problem. To offset the problems of physical security, companies will have to tighten their administrative security belts. This means that better controls and audits will have to be strongly enforced, and user-awareness seminars may need to be implemented.

Cost-Effectiveness

Across the industry, decision makers are stunned by the per-workstation cost in a computing environment. The goal is to determine what computing vehicle will deliver the most for your money. To do this, you must answer questions such as these:

- Is a microcomputer workstation cost-justified?
- How can a microcomputer be utilized for maximum cost-effectiveness?
- Would a minicomputer with connected terminals provide a superior solution?

Suppose, for example, that a manager is trying to determine whether to buy 30 microcomputers at $10,000 each or a $250,000 minicomputer system. The microcomputer will cost a total of $300,000 and will serve 30 users, whereas the minicomputers will cost $250,000, accommodate 50 users, and provide a means to share data and resources.

The evidence seems to indicate that the microcomputer approach isn't cost-justifiable. However, most end-users will prefer to work with microcomputer software rather than minicomputer-based software. The manager is faced with quite a problem. How do you propose a cost-effective system that will have high user acceptance and that will be integrated so that data and resources can be shared?

One possible solution to the problem of developing a cost-effective solution is to reduce the per-workstation cost of the microcomputer. This may mean purchasing monochrome instead of color monitors, for example.

Integration

Integration is the ability to tie the diverse resources of distributed processing into one functional system, while maintaining the benefits of a distributed environment. Organizations that use both a mainframe and microcomputers may be able to maximize the value of both systems through an integrated mainframe-micro link philosophy. Often companies want to tie the two major technologies, mainframes and micros, together through integrated hardware and software components. The vehicle for this integration will be not only software and hardware but also telecommunications. Telecommunications is the hub, or nucleus, of many mainframe-micro integration approaches.

The mainframe computing industry is backed by years of experience. Workable systems have been developed in areas such as telecommunications, security, backup and recovery, data administration, and management. If the microcomputer is properly integrated into the business environment, the knowledge gained using mainframe systems can be combined with micro technology to produce a superb integrated system.

SUMMARY

The mainframe-micro link has the potential to significantly improve a company's ability to process information. At the same time, it can lower the demands on the central data processing department and reduce the backlog of work hanging over most DP departments.

A microcomputer can be used for word processing, small database applications, graphics, financial analysis using spreadsheets, and many other functions. Much of the data used in these applications is stored in databases at central mainframe computers. Users of stand-alone micros must often rekey this information into their micro from mainframe-generated reports.

Mainframe-micro links can remove this intermediate step and provide a direct computer-to-computer transfer of information into microcomputer application software. This could save the time it takes to rekey data, reduce the likelihood of introducing errors during rekeying, and enable users to access the most up-to-date information.

2. The Intelligent Workstation

THE greatest resistance to microcomputers has come from traditional data processing departments. These departments want to see support, stability, and standardization before they invest heavily in any technology. Microcomputers have challenged these traditional approaches. The micro is a new type of machine that seems to thrive on nonstandardization — a machine that seems to have turned instability into a virtue.

MICROPROCESSORS: COMPUTERS ON A CHIP

The easiest way to classify computers is according to processing power. Modern computers get their processing capability from devices called microprocessors. A microprocessor, sometimes referred to as a processor, is a complex set of circuitry that is imprinted on a single silicon wafer, often smaller than a penny. Mainframe computers are equipped with many microprocessors. In some cases several microprocessors work simultaneously on different tasks. This is called *coprocessing.* The mainframe is also capable of using several microprocessors to complete a single task, a technique known as *parallel processing.*

Microcomputers generally have one microprocessor and are usually limited to doing one processing job at a time. (Notice the words *usually* and *generally*; a number of micros are now equipped with multiple microprocessors and can do co-processing.)

Minicomputers are somewhere between the micro and the mainframe: they have more processing power than a micro, but less than a mainframe. As microcomputers increase in power, however, the distinction between minis and micros is disappearing.

DIFFERENCES AMONG MICROCOMPUTERS

Micros are called *home computers, personal computers, microcomputers,* or *intelligent workstations.* In the area of micro-to-mainframe systems, the differences among micros are especially noticeable. Some microcomputers can be easily attached to a mainframe, while others are totally unsuitable for anything more than personal computing.

Before the mainframe-to-micro connection can be considered, it is necessary to identify exactly what kinds of microcomputers are available and how to select the right microcomputer for the application.

PROCESSOR SPEED

Microprocessors are not all equal. Their ability to process and transmit data varies considerably. This ability is measured in bits handled simultaneously. If a microprocessor can process 8 bits at once and can also transmit 8 bits at once, it is referred to as an *8-bit microprocessor.*

The Apple II and many other micros that followed it use an 8-bit central processing unit (CPU). Eight-bit technology is acceptable for home, school, and limited business functions, but limitations in the amount of data that such machines can handle make them less attractive as business machines. So, early in the 1980s, 8-bit machines for business were edged out by a new generation of 16-bit microcomputers. The 16-bit microcomputers can manipulate much larger batches of data and do much more complex processing than is practical on the slower 8-bit machines. Software developers use this increased power to create more sophisticated applications software packages.

Two primary types of 16-bit processors are in common use. One type can process data 16 bits at a time but can receive and transmit (input/output) data only 8 bits at a time. These processors are called *16/8-bit devices*; the Intel 8088 used in the IBM Personal Computer is a 16/8 chip. So-called "true" 16-bit processors, such as the Intel 8086, can handle processing and input/output in 16-bit sets. This makes them two to four times faster than 16/8 processors in terms of overall performance.

More powerful microcomputers are now equipped with a variety of 16/16-bit processors, such as the Intel 80186 and the 80286. These microprocessors are often used in machines equipped with one or more megabytes of electronic memory, or random-access memory (RAM).

The 16-bit microcomputer is being pushed by 32-bit technology, especially the Motorola MC68000. This chip is found on such products as the IBM AT-370, DEC Micro VAX, Apple Macintosh, and several others. Major manufacturers, however, seem intent on providing a full line of 16-bit as well as 32-bit products for the foreseeable future.

DESIGNING A WORKSTATION

Configuring the microcomputer to fit the end-user requirements is an important aspect of using microcomputers. Microcomputers come with a variety of capabilities; no single configuration fits all needs. The best approach is to study end-user requirements and fit the micro around these needs. For example, a workstation configuration for a secretary could probably be different from a configuration for a financial analyst.

When a microcomputer workstation is designed, what microprocessor to use is only one of several choices that must be made. Other areas, such as available memory (RAM), must also be analyzed.

RAM

Microcomputers have an electronic memory area called *random access memory* (RAM). The micro can process data only if the data is held in RAM. Thus, the amount of RAM determines the size and sophistication of applications programs and the size of files that the micro can process. Microcomputers today are offered with anywhere from 48 kilobytes (KB) of RAM to 3 megabytes (MB) or more of RAM. In general, office machines used primarily for word processing may need as little as 256KB of RAM. Micros used for spreadsheet analysis, program development, or graphics often need at least 512KB of RAM.

Many applications have a voracious appetite for memory and will readily use all that is available. This is particularly true when the application involves manipulating large quantities of data. Yet, purchasing micros with excess memory and/or storage may encourage inefficient use of the micro and communications networks. Making an economical and practical decision when buying RAM is not easy.

Disk Drives

Long-term storage on microcomputers is usually in the form of magnetic disks, which are either removable, as in the case of floppy disks, or fixed, as in the case of hard disks. Microcomputers can be equipped with one or more hard or floppy disk drives or with no disk drives at all.

Floppy disks normally hold from 160KB of data up to 1.2KB of data or more. Internal hard disks, those that use the micro's power supply and that fit within the micro chassis, typically hold from 5MB to 20MB of data. Floppy disk drives are less expensive; hard disk drives are more expensive, but are also faster and more convenient. Most microcomputers are equipped with at least one floppy disk drive. The choice of a second drive depends upon the uses of the individual workstation.

Expansion Bus

Larger microcomputers are frequently equipped with an expansion bus. The bus is a set of sockets into which special-purpose circuit boards can be inserted. An expansion bus with several available slots makes the microcomputer more adaptable to individual needs. Also, an expansion bus can encourage third parties to develop a variety of useful add-on products. Examples of add-on products that could plug into into the expansion bus include an internal modem, graphics cards, a voice digitizer, and local area network cards.

Many products that provide a mainframe-to-micro link require an expansion bus on the micro in order to connect the micro into a communications network. Along with the expansion bus, the microcomputer architecture must provide a sufficient number of communication port *addresses* to meet the needs of the particular workstation. Communication ports are logical channels out of the micro and are not related to the number of expansion slots. Such ports can be critical in workstation implementation. For example, you may not be able to successfully connect a local area network, a telephone modem, and a terminal-emulation card to a microcomputer if there are only two communication ports. (Local area networks, modems, and terminal emulation are covered in detail in later chapters.)

Communications Capability

Communications capability may refer to the type of output (communication protocol), the type of transmission line (serial or parallel), or the number of supportable workstations (as in multiuser systems). Micros with expansion buses usually can be adapted to any common protocol or transmission line. Supportable workstations depend upon the microprocessor being used and upon the operating system installed on the micro.

Operating System

The operating system is software that provides an interface between the applications software and the computer hardware. Operating systems may be single-user or multiuser. A single-user system supports one user; most stand-alone microcomputers use a single-user operating system. A multiuser operating system can run on a micro, a mini, or a mainframe. The system permits a machine's processor and other resources to be shared by attached terminals or micros.

MS-DOS, developed by Microsoft, is the standard single-user operating system for many 16-bit microcomputers. Software developers can write applications to run on MS-DOS, with only slight modifications for specific hardware.

UNIX, a product of Bell Laboratories, is an often-used multiuser operating system. Modified versions of UNIX, such as XE-NIX, have commands and features similar to UNIX and have been adapted for many different microcomputers.

A MULTIFUNCTION INTELLIGENT WORKSTATION

The personal computer has achieved much of its success through its multipurpose nature. Traditional workstations, such as terminals and dedicated word processors, tend to be single-purpose. In comparison, the microcomputer can emulate virtually any traditional workstation task and can also perform many tasks hitherto unavailable at a personal workstation. Properly used, the micro can be highly cost-effective as a multifunction device (see figure 2–1).

To achieve cost-effectiveness, an intelligent workstation should perform multiple tasks, be easy to use, and be designed around the users' needs. The microcomputer can deliver a multitude of services to the user. Ease of use is a matter of personal interpretation. However, some simple tests are generally accepted for determining the ease of use of software products. Easy-to-use software should provide on-line help, good documentation, simple keystroke commands, and a means for using menus or icons.

Menu-driven software has options clearly stated on a menu screen, and using the program requires no in-depth knowledge

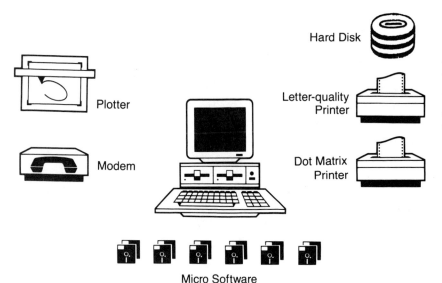

FIGURE 2–I: *One of the strong appeals of the microcomputer is its ability to control many automated services, including plotting, printing, and various types of software applications.*

of the software or of computer programming. In addition, the software should allow experienced users to skip past the menus they no longer need. As an alternative to menus, some software uses icons, which are graphic pictures representing various functions. To select a function, you usually must place a pointer on the proper icon. In some instances, icons are much faster to use than menus. Xerox and Apple Computer have been pioneers in the field of icon processing. One of the major concerns when icon processing is used is the amount of CPU processing necessary to create pictures of desired functions.

WINDOWING AND INTEGRATED SOFTWARE

Some jobs require people to switch from one task to another; the micro user can be equipped with software that allows the user to do this. For example, a person could be using a word processor, switch out of the word processor to search for and retrieve related information from a database, then return to the same place in the word processor to enter the information.

Two software techniques permit switching smoothly from one application to another. One is *windowing*, in which several different applications may be loaded into RAM simultaneously. Each of these applications is assigned a specific area, or window, within the micro's display screen. Thus, the user has access to several applications simultaneously. Microsoft Windows, DESQ (Quarterdeck), and Topview (IBM) are examples of windowing products.

Another technique used for switching between applications is available with integrated software. Integrated software is a set of different software applications that allows data to be passed back and forth from one application to another. An integrated package might include a word processor, a database manager, a spreadsheet, and a graphics program. Three widely used integrated products of this type are Symphony, from Lotus Development Corporation; Framework, from Ashton-Tate; and Mac Switcher, from Apple Computer.

In an integrated system, data from the spreadsheet can be converted directly into a graph, and the graph can then be integrated within a document prepared by the word processor. Some integrated packages are so sophisticated that changing data stored in one format will automatically change identical data stored in another format. In other words, if spreadsheet figures are changed, the related graph changes automatically. Integrated software packages may or may not include windowing as a feature.

THE SUPERMICRO

A supermicro is a powerful microcomputer that operates on a 16-bit or 32-bit processor. In addition to a high-end processor, supermicros are normally equipped with more RAM and greater disk storage than standard microcomputers. Frequently, supermicros have improved communications capabilities; these can be used to integrate the supermicro into a large communications network and also to support multiple terminals and additional micros.

Most supermicros can run at least one single-user operating system and one multiuser operating system, but usually not at the same time. In its multiuser configuration, the supermicro performs the processing for itself and for attached terminals. In other words, the supermicro provides the intelligence for the system and serves as coordinator or facilitator of system activities.

Supermicros also work well as part of a local area network (LAN). In a LAN, intelligent workstations are connected to share information and services, but each workstation performs its own processing. Nonetheless, some administrative and management processing must be performed on the LAN to coordinate activities, and the supermicro handles this role well.

The supermicro is not a new technology. It has been used for several years in scientific and engineering environments for computer-aided design (CAD) and computer-aided manufacturing (CAM). In order to perform these tasks, the supermicro had to possess extreme power and flexibility. Now this power and flexibility is migrating into the hands of business professionals.

Overall, the supermicro can blend well with current microcomputer products. However, it is not necessarily a replacement for the low-end microcomputer. Most people don't need the power of a supermicro on their desks. The selection of a super-micro should be based on user needs.

A number of manufacturers offer supermicros. Tables 2–1 through 2–4 summarize the features of supermicros from IBM, Digital Equipment Corporation, Hewlett-Packard, and AT&T.

TABLE 2–I.

Features of IBM's Supermicros

FEATURE	SUPERMICRO		
	AT	AT-370	9000
Processor(s)			
8088 (16/8 Bit)	—	Std.	—
8087 (Math Coprocessor)	—	Std.	—
80286 (32/16 Bit)	Std.	Std.	—
80287 (Math Coprocessor)	Opt.	Opt.	—
68000 (32 Bit)	—	Std.	Std.
Operating System	DOS 3.X	DOS 3.X	CSOS
	—	—	
	XENIX	XENIX	XENIX
	—	VM/CMS	UNIX
Memory			
Standard Config.	512KB	256KB	640KB
Maximum Config.	3MB	3MB	5MB
Multiuser			
Maximum Number of Users	3	—	—
Communications			
Async	Opt.	Opt.	Std.
Bisync	Opt.	Opt.	Opt.
SNA	Opt.	Opt.	Opt.
Floppy Disk Drive			
360KB	Std.	Std.	Std.
1.2MB	Std.	Std.	—
Fixed Disk			
10MB	—	Std.	Opt.
20MB	Opt.	Opt.	Opt.
40MB	Opt.	Opt.	Opt.

TABLE 2—2.

Features of DEC's Supermicros

FEATURE	SUPERMICRO	
	MICRO VAX I	MICRO PDP-11
Processor		
68000 (32 Bit)	Std.	Std.
Operating System		
RSTS/E		Opt.
UNIX	Opt.	Opt.
RT-11		Opt.
VMS	Opt.	—
Memory		
Standard Config.	1.0MB	256KB
Maximum Config.	2.5MB	4MB
Cache	8K	—
Virtual	4GB	—
Multiuser		
Maximum Number of Users	4	10
Communications		
X.25	Opt.	Opt.
SNA	Opt.	Opt.
DECNET	Opt.	Opt.
ETHERNET	Opt.	Opt.
SYNC	Opt.	Opt.
ASYNC	Std.	Std.
Floppy Disk Drive		
800KB	Std.	Std.
Fixed Disk		
10MB	—	Std.
28MB	Std.	Opt.

IBM XT/AT-370

The XT/AT-370 personal computer is one of IBM's more power-ful workstations. It has the ability to support three central pro-cessing units, two 16-bit CPUs, and one 32-bit CPU. A particu-lar specialty is its ability to run VM/CMS, an IBM mainframe operating system. This machine is the only IBM microcomputer that has this ability and is the only IBM micro that can run

TABLE 2—3.

Features of HP's Supermicro	
FEATURE	HP 9000
Processor	
68000 (32 Bit)	Std.
Operating System	
HP-UX	Std.
UNIX	Opt.
Memory	
Standard Config.	2.5MB
Maximum Config.	2.5MB
Multiuser	
Maximum Number of Users	6
Communications	
Async	Opt.
Sync	Opt.
Floppy Disk Drive	
630KB	Std.
Hard Disk	
4.6MB	Std.
14.5MB	Opt.

mainframe software "as-is." Thus it has mainframe integration capabilities unmatched by any other IBM microcomputer.

Furthermore, the XT/AT-370 has advantages in the area of applications-program development. Because the unit has the power and the capability to run mainframe software, it can be used as a stand-alone development tool, reducing the load of the mainframe.

A word of caution is needed here, however. The XT/AT-370 is an extremely powerful workstation designed for large business and engineering applications. The machine should not be viewed as a general-purpose workstation for end-users.

IBM PC/AT

The IBM PC/AT is IBM's first supermicro aimed at the business professional. It is designed to increase productivity through high-speed processors, an improved keyboard, and increased

TABLE 2—4.

Features of AT&T's Supermicro

FEATURE	3B2
Processor	
68000 (32 Bit)	Std.
Operating System	
UNIX	Std.
MS-DOS	Opt.
Memory	
Standard Config.	512KB
Maximum Config.	1MB
Multiuser	
Maximum Number of Users	6
Communications	
Async	Std.
Sync	Opt.
Floppy Disk	
720KB	Std.
Fixed Disk	
10MB	Std.
32MB	Opt.

memory space. For its CPU, the AT uses the 80286 and the optional 80287 numeric coprocessor. Operationally, it has two to three times the computing speed of the IBM PC and IBM XT. The unit will accommodate up to 3MB of RAM and up to 41.2MB of disk storage.

The power and storage capabilities of the AT allow it to be a multitasking machine, which means that multiple applications (tasks) can run concurrently. It can even serve as a multitasking/multiuser system, handling the processing for as many as three workstations. Besides its potential as a powerful stand-alone and multiuser system, the AT is also an excellent network server for local area networks (see chapter 15). In this capacity, the AT can function as the manager of central storage, as a communications gateway, and as coordinator of activities for attached microcomputers. Like other supermicros, the AT can provide these services and still have enough residual processing power to simultaneously function as a personal workstation.

IBM 9000

The IBM 9000 is primarily an engineering workstation. The machine operates on a 32-bit processor running the UNIX operating system. In the engineering environment, the 9000 is used for computer-aided design (CAD) and high-speed numeric computations. The 9000 was not designed for the business world and thus should not be considered as a workstation for that environment. The engineering performance of this unit is often compared to similar products offered by DEC and HP. High-speed simulation and high-quality graphics are among the better features of the 9000.

Digital Equipment Corporation Micro VAX

The Micro VAX was one of the first supermicros on the market. It is a small unit packed with superb power. This 32-bit supermicro is designed to be compatible with VAX architecture and performance. The Digital Equipment Corporation (DEC) VAX series is widely used throughout the industry. The Micro VAX benefits from its compatibility with the larger VAX computers and can run the many software programs written for the VAX series. The VMS and UNIX operating systems run on both the low-end Micro VAX and the larger VAX systems.

The Micro VAX will integrate exceptionally well into those business environments that use large DEC systems. In addition to its multiuser capabilities, the Micro VAX has been used frequently as a network server on Ethernet-type LANs. The architecture of the Micro VAX gives it high-performance network capabilities far beyond many other supermicros.

The DEC Micro PDP-11

The Micro PDP-11 follows the same design principles as the Micro VAX. It is designed to be fully compatible with larger PDP systems. This supermicro operates on the same operating systems as larger DEC minicomputers. The Micro PDP-11 will support several DEC workstations and serve as a communications gateway to other systems. The PDP-11 runs several multiuser software programs and operates on DEC's DECNET network.

Hewlett-Packard 9000

The HP 9000 (see figure 2–2) was one of the first supermicros and was actually on the market before the term *supermicro* appeared. The HP 9000 is based on a proprietary 32-bit processor developed by Hewlett-Packard. The HP 9000 can, in effect, serve as three computers simultaneously. This is accomplished through "plug-in CPU" technology. Each circuit card contains its own 32-bit processor and associated circuitry, allowing the HP 9000 to perform several tasks simultaneously.

The HP 9000 is used in a variety of environments, including business, education, engineering, and manufacturing. Because the 9000 possesses multiple 32-bit processors and the HP-UX operating system (a version of UNIX), the 9000 has been adopted

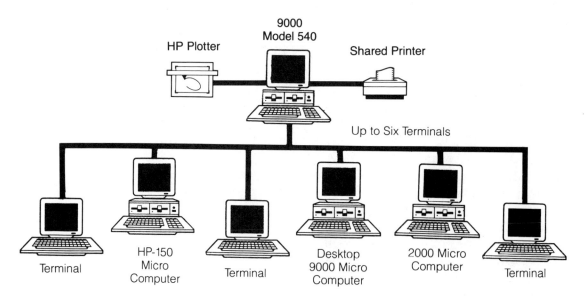

FIGURE 2–2: *The HP 9000 is a high-speed numerical processing supermicro, capable of supporting various workstations and peripherals.*

primarily by the engineering and manufacturing communities. The 9000 is capable of very high speed number crunching, as well as computer-aided design. The system supports such programming languages as COBOL, FORTRAN, Pascal, and several others.

The recent increased interest in factory automation has opened the door for many computer manufacturers and the HP 9000 has moved swiftly into the manufacturing field. The HP 9000's popularity in this area is largely attributed to its performance and the innovative software being developed by Hewlett-Packard along with other sources.

The HP 9000 is not targeted for the business community as much as it is for science, engineering, and manufacturing.

AT&T 3B2

The break-up of AT&T has permitted AT&T to enter the competitive computer industry. Although new to the commercial computer market, AT&T is not new to computers or communications. AT&T's version of a supermicro is the 3B2 system (see figure 2–3), centered around a 32-bit processor and the UNIX operating system.

UNIX is an important ingredient in the 3B2 and to AT&T as a whole. The operating system was designed at AT&T's Bell Laboratories to be used internally within the lab's own scientific environment. UNIX proved to be a powerful and versatile multiuser operating system. As the outside world began to hear about UNIX, interest in the product grew. As a result of popular demand, Bell Labs began licensing the operating system externally. Since that time UNIX has grown to be one of the leading multiuser operating systems.

The 3B2 supermicro is a high-performance system that can simultaneously serve from one to six users. Besides serving multiple users, the 3B2 offers such capabilities as printer sharing, hard-disk sharing, and shared communications. The 3B2 also supports a variety of terminals, as well as AT&T and IBM microcomputers.

The 3B2 also supports some advanced features, such as concurrent dual operating systems. For example, the 3B2 can support the MS-DOS operating system running underneath UNIX.

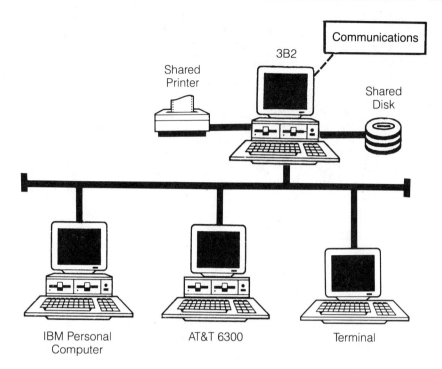

FIGURE 2–3: *Because the AT&T supermicro supports both UNIX and MS-DOS, a company can integrate both IBM and AT&T products within a common network.*

This allows the 3B2 to run not only thousands of UNIX-based programs but also programs written for MS-DOS.

In summary, the combination of the 32-bit processor, UNIX and MS-DOS operating systems, multiuser capabilities, and shared resources make the 3B2 a strong contender in the supermicro area.

SUMMARY

The term *microcomputer* is used throughout this book to refer to small computers with certain similar characteristics. However, micros come in a variety of configurations and capabilities.

The actual choice of a microcomputer workstation should be based on end-user requirements, your overall computing environment and the strategic direction set forth by your company and your most widely used vendor.

3. Linking Minicomputers to Microcomputers

AS has been explained, micro, supermicro, mini, and mainframe computers are differentiated by their relative power and design characteristics (see figure 3–1). In the selection of a data processing system, the goal is to select the proper machine to fit particular organizational requirements.

The minicomputer is situated between the micro and mainframe in size, processing power, and cost. These versatile machines can serve as host computers to workstations in medium to small companies. In large companies, they are often the *departmental host*, a complex function that will be discussed later in this chapter.

CAPABILITIES OF MINICOMPUTERS

Minicomputers typically have at least one very fast CPU and may be able to serve as many as 60 users simultaneously. User requests are answered sequentially, but with such speed that the user perceives no significant delay in processing.

The trend now is to put distributed, dedicated processors on the minicomputer. For instance, one 16-bit processor may be used to handle communications, another to handle only input/output, and another to handle general processing. On some

Microcomputer:
1 User

FIGURE 3–1: *The different computing levels all have a place within the corporate environment. The actual choice of equipment is dependent upon the number of users to be served.*

Supermicro:
3–10 Users

Departmental Minicomputer:
100 or Fewer Users

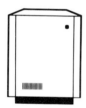

Minicomputer:
1000 or Fewer Users

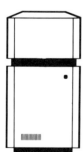

Mainframe:
Several Thousand Users

minicomputers, a processor is assigned to do nothing more than check keystrokes. For example, if you have defined a field to be numeric and subsequently try to enter a letter in that field, the terminal will beep and not allow the entry. The keystroke-checking processor on the mini will find the prohibited character and reject it. This checking procedure is common to many machines.

All of the basic functions that require significant processing time may be assigned their own dedicated processors. This relieves the central processing unit (CPU) of all of the machine and data-movement chores, leaving it free to handle actual processing. Overall, this approach can make the throughput of a minicomputer system much faster.

MINI OR MICRO HOST

Both the minicomputer and the micro can be used as host computers in a multiuser system. For example, an order-entry system often has one central database that is accessed and manipulated by several users. A single central computing device must manage all the requests funneling into the single database; that device could be a mini or a microcomputer.

In most cases, the management of a multiuser system should be given to a minicomputer or, for large applications, a mainframe. Like mainframe computers, most minis are designed to be multiuser. Microcomputers, on the other hand, tend to be single-user. The micro can be adapted to multiuser functions, such as acting as a network server on a local area network, but when several users simultaneously use a microcomputer as a host for multiuser processing, the throughput typically slows to an unacceptable level. The microcomputer can serve one user at a time, whereas the minicomputer can typically accommodate between 6 and 100 users. Besides power, some other differences between minis and micros are important when the computer is to play the role of multiuser host. Table 3–1 lists some of the differences between the two computing environments.

TABLE 3–1.

Comparison of Minicomputers and Microcomputers

Advantages

MINICOMPUTER	MICROCOMPUTER
1. Can Share Peripherals	1. Low Start-up Cost
2. Can Interconnect Several Users	2. Easy-to-use Software
3. Can Share Communications	3. Available Software Often Meets Personal Requirements
4. Can Process Several Requests Simultaneously Using the Same Data Elements	

Disadvantages

MINICOMPUTER	MICROCOMPUTER
1. High Cost per User for Small Installations	1. High Cost per User for Large Installations
2. Applications Are Often General in Nature Compared to Alternatives	2. Limited Multiuser Capabilities

LINKING THE TECHNOLOGIES

A minicomputer with several attached microcomputers creates a powerful computing combination. In an office environment, such things as ease-of-use, integration, resource sharing, and reduced cost per workstation are important objectives. These objectives may be realized through a well-planned mini-micro integrated solution.

Connecting several microcomputers to a minicomputer system lets the microcomputer user share peripherals and data. These peripherals might include devices such as high-speed printers and plotters. In addition to connecting devices, a minicomputer can also serve as a communications gateway to larger systems.

As an illustration of how companies can benefit from peripheral sharing, consider a company in which microcomputer users frequently need a modem. Say that these modems cost $300 each. If every micro is supplied with a modem and there are 30 microcomputers, this represents a $9,000 investment in modems. Typically, the majority of these modems will sit idle. With a minicomputer system, several modems can be attached to the system and shared among users. The number of modems can be reduced dramatically using the shared modem concept. The same 30 microcomputer users might be able to operate with a modem pool of 10 modems, which would represent a reduction of $6,000 in modem cost.

In addition to shared communications, some minicomputers allow the microcomputer user to share the minicomputer disk storage (see figure 3–2). Shared storage is sometimes referred to as *virtual disk support*. Virtual disk sharing can represent a substantial cost reduction at the workstation level. In such an en-

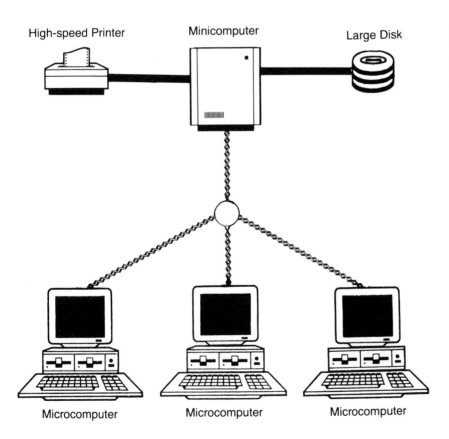

High-speed Printer   Minicomputer   Large Disk

Microcomputer   Microcomputer   Microcomputer

FIGURE 3–2: *Microcomputer storage can be centralized by interconnecting the micro with a departmental minicomputer.*

vironment, microcomputers without hard disks can be given to people and then linked to hard-disk operations on the mini. Equally important, this configuration can provide a means of controlling data, security, back-up, and recovery; it also helps control costs.

CONNECTING MINICOMPUTERS AND MICROS

Minicomputers are connected to micros in a variety of ways. Typically, each minicomputer manufacturer has a particular wiring scheme. The medium is usually a coaxial cable connected to the minicomputer and run to each microcomputer, terminal, or printer.

Minicomputers were originally designed to accommodate terminals, not microcomputers. Because of this, the method of connecting a microcomputer to a minicomputer is usually accomplished through a technique known as *terminal emulation.* Terminal emulation involves making the micro look like a terminal to a host mini system. The electronic deception is performed with emulation software and an emulator circuit board. Emulating a specific terminal enables the microcomputer to gain access to the minicomputer system.

Most office minicomputer systems also permit outside dial-up access, thus allowing a remote micro user to connect to a centralized minicomputer. To accomplish this, the user needs a simple modem and appropriate communications software.

Because of the flexible communication options found on many minicomputers, an office environment can be equipped with a combination of terminals, microcomputers, plotters, and printers, all interconnected on one system. The following case studies illustrate some of the various configurations that can be used.

Case 1

A stock brokerage firm uses a minicomputer to manage a centralized database. Often several brokers will query the database simultaneously, which requires the faster minicomputer processing capability (as compared to that of a micro).

Each broker also has a microcomputer for local processing.

With this system, when a client asks, "What telecommunications stock is the best to buy right now?" the broker can call up the departmental database that contains this information. The broker can also use the microcomputer to produce financial analyses on clients' portfolios and to produce results based on different options. A micro spreadsheet program is ideal for this task.

In a case such as this, a blend of microcomputers and a shared minicomputer may be the best choice.

Case 2

An office has people who are doing financial modeling and graphics using their microcomputers. At the same time, secretaries are using terminals connected to the minicomputer for their word processing. The people doing local processing on microcomputers are connected to the mini system and are thus able to send their spreadsheets or other output to the minicomputer; the secretaries can then merge them with reports.

Here, a minicomputer serves both microcomputers and terminals.

Case 3

In larger companies in which enough data processing is done to require a large mainframe computer, the minicomputer system can be used at an intermediate point in the mainframe-micro link. A department could use a minicomputer with terminals or micro workstations. In such environments, the micro can function as a terminal to manipulate data on the mini. Alternatively, the micro can function in the microcomputer mode for local processing. Finally, the micro could use the communications capability of the mini to access the larger mainframe system.

Case 4

Consider a group of ten data entry clerks. Their primary job is to access and update a specific database. In this situation, a centralized device is needed to control database activities, and a minicomputer with terminals is ideal.

In this case, microcomputer workstations aren't needed for simple data entry and updating of the database. Because the minicomputer's CPU is doing all of the processing, terminal workstations are adequate. The point is that the micro is not the answer in every situation. Once again, user requirements should be the dictating force in selecting a workstation.

CASE SUMMARY

For information that needs to be accessed by many people simultaneously, a minicomputer offers a tremendous advantage. If your information requires access by only a few users in close proximity, then a microcomputer may be ideal. In addition, as was illustrated above, in some environments a combination of the two computer systems can be the best solution.

By attaching a microcomputer to the minicomputer, you can add much more flexibility. Data can be downloaded from the minicomputer and manipulated on the microcomputer in a variety of ways.

Throughout the rest of this book, when mainframe-micro links are discussed, virtually the same examples should apply to a mini-micro link environment.

MINICOMPUTERS AND MAINFRAMES

A minicomputer is often used in combination with mainframe computers and microcomputers. Let's examine this situation by looking at Company X. Company X is multidivisional, with a large central data processing department. Each division has several departments (see figure 3–3).

Within each department is a group of people who are using data on the mainframe. These people are not really in control of their data and are allowed only limited access because of the way the system software was designed. Putting a minicomputer in each department could allow for the downloading of needed data from the mainframe to the departmental mini. If this were accomplished, personnel within the department would have the flexibility to create reports and analyze data on the minicomputer. If the departmental minicomputer were linked with mi-

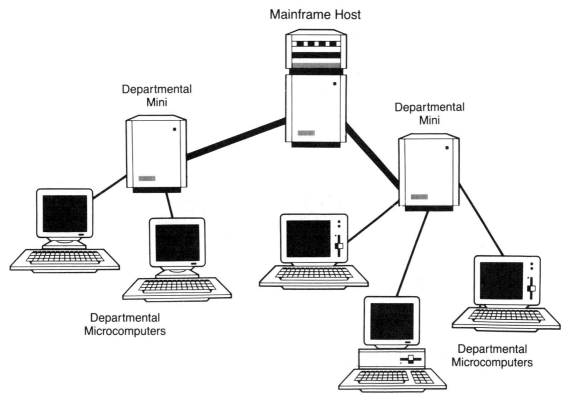

FIGURE 3–3: *Departmental minicomputers are a means of bringing computer services closer to the departmental users.*

cros, data from the mini could be further downloaded to a micro for additional processing.

COST AND THE MINICOMPUTER

Cost is also a factor in the decision to use a mini. Typically, departments are charged a fixed cost for the minicomputer. Once the computer is corporately paid for, departmental use of the mini is "free." When doing the same processing on a central mainframe, each bit of data manipulation results in a recurring cost. Because there is so much overhead in many DP organizations, the departments that use the mainframe are faced with never-ending cost. Using the minicomputer, you can bring down all of the data you need in one large transfer. Your only cost then is moving the data from the mainframe to the mini. The reporting and analysis against that data is essentially free. This type of approach is an alternative to traditional time-sharing use of a centralized mainframe.

Thus, a major reason that departments are starting to use the departmental mini as an intermediate device is to cut down the costs of interactive or on-line processing.

PRODUCT EXAMPLE: IBM'S SYSTEM/36

In the early 1980s, so much enthusiasm was generated by the microcomputer that minicomputers were often overlooked and undervalued. As the foregoing examples illustrate, the minicomputer can be an important element in corporate communications.

The System/36 is the successor to the successful System/34, a leader in departmental small systems. The System/36 builds on the success of the System/34 and is fully software compatible. The System/36 is strategically positioned among IBM's superminis, its 43XX systems, and its microcomputer line. The System/36 was designed not as a replacement for the superminis or microcomputers but rather as a complement to those environments. Additionally, the System/36 is also designed for those environments that the superminis or microcomputers cannot cost-effectively address.

Architecture of the System/36

One of the most important characteristics of the System/36 is the distributed processor design. The System/36 is equipped with a variety of 8-, 16-, and 32-bit processors. Each processor has a specific task or tasks. For instance, one processor handles communications, another manages input and output, and another performs general processing.

The System/36 comes in three configurations, the model 5360, the 5362, and the 5364 desktop model. The chief difference between the two is capacity. Capacity is measured by such things as maximum number of stations, available disk storage, and memory.

Workstation Support

The IBM System/36 is flexible in that it supports a variety of terminals, microcomputers, printers, and plotters. These devices are interconnected via a twinax cabling scheme. The combination of the cabling and operating system allows all the devices on a System/36 to communicate with one another. For example, a microcomputer attached to a System/36 could print a document on a letter-quality printer located on a different floor. This sharing of resources, such as printers, can do much to reduce peripheral cost.

Software

When a computer, such as the System/36, is designed for small departments, nontechnical users, and office automation, software becomes critical for market acceptance. Two factors have helped the System/36 in the software area. First, as mentioned before, the System/36 is software and hardware compatible with the early System/34. Because of this, a tremendous amount of software already exists for the System/36. This software spans such areas as office automation, accounting, graphics, database management, finance, and many other areas. There is also an enormous amount of software available in vertical markets, such as medical, dental, retail, and so on. In these environments, as well as others, the System/36 is considered a solution system.

Microcomputer Support

The System/36 supports local cable-attached and remote dial-up IBM microcomputers. A local micro is connected to the System/36 via a card plugged into the microcomputer. This card serves two purposes: it allows the cable that comes from the System/36 to be connected to the microcomputer, and it allows the microcomputer to emulate a System/36 terminal, thus giving the micro user full access to the System/36. The micro user has all the functionality of the microcomputer, plus the added features of the System/36.

Another plus for microcomputer users connected to the System/36 is *virtual disk space.* This feature allows an IBM microcomputer to use the vast storage of the System/36 as logical disk space for the micro. For example, if a user has an IBM PC with two floppy disk drives connected to a System/36, that user can access a 32MB simulated micro hard disk on the System/36. This capability eliminates the need to equip each user with a stand-alone hard disk. The System/36 virtual micro hard disk is treated as drive C, D, etc.

Telecommunications

The IBM System/36 supports a host of communications options. It can be linked to other System/36s or larger computer systems, both IBM and non-IBM. The communication tie to other systems is supported through such bisynchronous protocols as SNA/SDLC and X.25, and asynchronously via protocol converters.

In a departmental situation, the System/36 can be programmed to automatically connect (*autocall*) to a larger mainframe during off-hours and bring data down for later use. The communications capabilities of the System/36 are shared among all devices on the system, both terminals and microcomputers. For example, there is no need to buy individual modems for microcomputers. Because the micro is attached to the System/36, it can use the modems available at the System/36 as if they were locally attached.

SUMMARY

The IBM System/36 appears to have strategic importance that may affect the future of office automation. It is designed to work well in environments with microcomputers. A well-planned implementation of microcomputers and terminals around a System/36 can be a cost-effective, integrated environment.

The communications available on the System/36 provide the needed flexibility to connect the System/36 to larger systems or other System/36s. This is the kind of flexibility needed to ease the problem of integrating the mainframe and desktop computers.

4. The Corporate Database

THE subject of databases is enormous and complex — and far beyond the scope of this book. Nonetheless, you should understand certain database terms and concepts that are fundamental to the mainframe-micro environment. The material in this chapter deals exclusively with the most common mainframe databasees.

The ability to access and manipulate mainframe data is crucial to the success of the microcomputer in the corporate environment. Excellent mainframe-micro link software is now available. Using this software to access the corporate database enables micro users to produce flexible reports in the format needed for subsequent analyses.

People who use the corporate database for analyses usually see only fragments of the database in printed reports. Reports represent selected portions of information that have been put into usable form by a computer programmer. Thus, most people have little understanding of the *structure* of the database. However, effective use of the corporate database from a microcomputer requires an understanding of the database structure.

DATABASE FUNDAMENTALS

A *database* is any organized collection of information. It may provide the raw material from which reports can be written, analyses made, and plans developed, or it may be as simple as a telephone directory, providing only basic reference information.

Databases are not restricted to any particular type of storage media, although increasingly data are stored on magnetic disks. Magnetic media are only moderately stable storage vehicles; that is, data on magnetic media can be lost or damaged more easily than if they were stored on paper (called *hard copy*). The popularity of magnetic storage is due to its compactness and its compatibility with electronic storage. Data passes easily from magnetic storage to electronic storage, a necessary step in order for the data to be accessed and manipulated by computers.

Usually a database is comprised of related information. For example, personnel records and sales reports would be stored in different databases. Separation into related sets of data simplifies

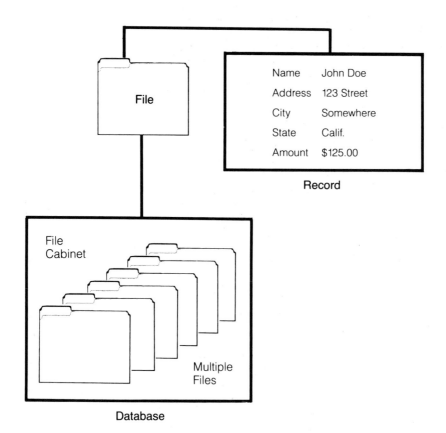

FIGURE 4–1: *Information in a database is broken down into files and records.*

the retrieval process. It also makes it easier to prevent unauthorized access to data.

The most common physical representation of a database is the company file cabinet (see figure 4–1). The database, like the file cabinet, holds a large amount of data that is divided into smaller and more narrowly defined collections of information called *files*. Within the files are particular entries called *records*. Each record contains *fields*. Typical fields can be such elements as account number, name, month, and so forth. Fields are important components of a database because they provide a means of comparing, selecting, and sorting the data. If you want to retrieve a list of names of all of your customers, for example, you would request the full list of all name fields for each record.

DATABASE STRUCTURES

In non-computerized offices, a prime component of efficiency is a "good filing system." The phrase implies a system that lets you store and retrieve data easily, but there is no single, universally acceptable filing system. A system must be tailored for each situation.

The same variety of filing systems is necessary in computerized offices. The computerized filing system, or *database structure*, should be selected so that it matches the type of information, the technical level of the personnel, and the size and power of the computing system being used. In large computerized organizations, three major database structures are in common use: *hierarchical*, *relational*, and *network*.

Hierarchical Database

Of these three database structures, the hierarchical database is the most widely used in corporations. A hierarchical database, such as IMS (IBM's Information Management System), resembles an inverted tree structure with elements and subelements branching outward from the center. Each limb of the tree is part of the path through related data to specific files and records.

The concept of *paths* is fundamental to hierarchical databases. As data are more narrowly defined, the paths branch away from data that are unrelated at a given level (see figure 4–2). Ap-

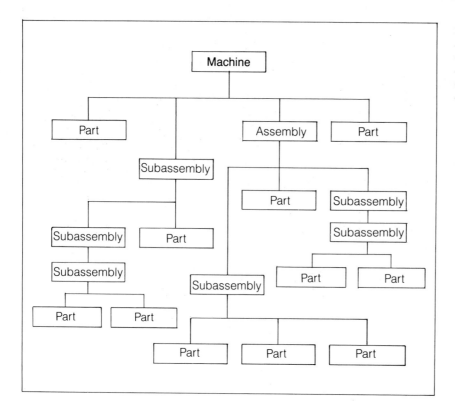

plying the hierarchical system to a sales organization, for example, underneath the database title "Sales," the path might branch to "Eastern sales" and "Western sales." The path below Eastern sales might branch to "Commercial sales" and "Government sales."

The benefit of this type of structure is that unrelated data can be ignored by the computer. Retrieving information on government sales in the Eastern region is a three-step process: Sales to Eastern sales to Government sales.

One of the drawbacks of a hierarchical structure is that data can be difficult to locate. If you're searching for the total sales made by salesman Smith, you must know his region and type of sales. Otherwise, you must search each path until you eventually find Smith.

Another drawback concerns people who need to retrieve data from widely divergent paths. A computer can search quickly through subelements beneath a single element. Even at electronic processing speeds, however, significant amounts of time can be lost going from a sub-element on one path to a sub-element on another path. Like a human traveler, the computer must retrace the old path to the point where the old and new paths branch, then follow the new path down to the required sub-subelement.

A hierarchical database can be many levels deep, with many branches at each level. The hierarchical technique was designed to accommodate large and complex database requirements; however, because of innovative advances in modern DBMS software programs, a user's view of the hierarchical database can be greatly simplified. These DBMS programs allow the user to view a specific level, branch, or field.

Developing a hierarchical database will typically require advanced professional data processing personnel to realign or modify the database. The hierarchical database system is one of the older approaches to database management, but is an efficient and flexible means of resource utilization on a mainframe computer.

Relational Database

The relational database, a second common structure, stores information in a row-and-column format (see figure 4–3). Nontechnical users, who might avoid using more complex types of databases, are apt to use a relational database because of its simplicity and easily understood design. (Actual ease of use varies among specific software programs; however, relational databases are generally less complex than hierarchical databases.)

ID Number	Name	Department	Division
16434	John Smith	24	A
26421	Sue Jacobs	38	B
31614	Kevin Wallace	47	C

FIGURE 4–3: *Data in a relational database are stored in a row-and-column format.*

The relational method is rapidly becoming the most popular database storage technique. The row-and-column format has made the relational approach adaptable to micro-based software, such as dBASE III by Ashton Tate. On the mainframe, relational databases are found in such software as FOCUS, RAMIS, IDMS/R, and many others.

When large amounts of data are involved, the relational database offers less flexibility than the hierarchical or network approaches. Large or complex databases are usually organized using the hierarchical or network models. However, a hierarchical networked database can be designed to present a relational view. Cullinet's IDMS and IDMS/R are examples of this approach, offering the system developer the power of a network DBMS while still offering nontechnical people an easy-to-use relational database interface.

Network Database

A third common storage structure is the network database (see figure 4–4). The network database provides the programmer with the flexibility and power of the hierarchical database, while giving the appearance of a relational database.

The network method is similar to the hierarchical approach in its use of records and paths. The basic difference in the two approaches is that the hierarchical model supports *one-to-many* relationships, whereas the network approach supports *many-to-many* relationships. Either approach requires people to navigate through the data relationships to retrieve or view information.

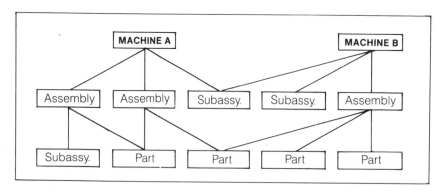

FIGURE 4–4: *A network database is designed to support cross-relationships among multiple files or databases.*

Usually, the navigating is performed by a computer programmer, who produces a report that presents the information in a way that is usable by others. The trend today, however, is toward simplification of the database structure, so that nondata-processing personnel can find data and produce useful reports. This approach is widely referred to as *user-friendly interfaces.* However, the actual degree of user friendliness a product offers is highly subjective.

A network approach can tie several hierarchical databases together. The person using the databases sees only a single, logical view of the data, even though the data may be distributed across many databases. For instance, a user may be accessing five or six different databases in order to generate one report. The benefit of a network approach is that the complexity of dealing with multiple databases is handled by the network system's software.

Becoming familiar with the three basic corporate database structures — hierarchical, relational, and network — enables you to understand how to access these databases, an important key to the success of a mainframe-micro link.

DATABASE MANAGEMENT SYSTEM (DBMS)

Whatever actual structure is used, all databases are part of a database management system. A database management system is a system of software tools used to control the creation of, access to, and modification of information in the database (see figure 4–5). The DBMS acts as the custodian for all data in the database.

ACCESSING THE DATABASE

The purpose of creating a mainframe-micro link is to provide access to data. At the same time, DP managers strive to reduce access costs while maintaining the integrity and security of the data residing in the mainframe.

Several issues must be addressed before people are allowed to access information from a corporate database. The size of mainframe database files may make it difficult to download files into a microcomputer. The speed with which the files need to be

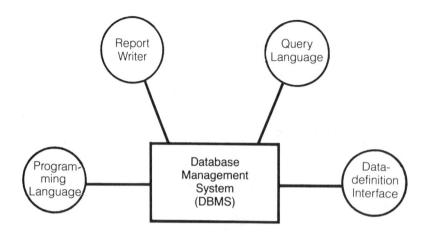

FIGURE 4–5: *The database management system is the custodian of the database. Input and output of information to a DBMS is performed through programming, the report writer, queries, and the data-definition interface.*

transferred must also be considered. Additionally, a company must decide whether to allow users to manipulate the data at the microcomputer and upload the changes into the mainframe ("read/modify") or to provide a "read-only" system that enables users to download data only for analysis and production of reports.

The first issues, the size of the database, can be handled by summarizing the data at the mainframe before downloading to micros. Microcomputer software and hardware may not be able to handle the tremendous number of detail records stored in a large corporate database, but those data can be summarized into a more manageable size. A good mainframe-micro link package should provide an automatic checking mechanism for the size of the file and should indicate if the file is too large to transfer. The mainframe-micro package should also allow you to qualify the data extraction requirements, thus minimizing the number of records to be downloaded into the micro.

The question of the speed of transfer can be addressed through the mainframe-micro package's ability to provide for both immediate access and batch processing. Batch processing enables the user to process information during scheduled times.

The next issue to resolve is whether to provide read-only (query) or read/modify (extraction) access. This issue involves the question of data integrity. Access and security issues must be resolved by each individual corporation. However, a mainframe-micro package should enable you to indicate or specify whether files or databases are read-only or read/modify.

A read-only (query) system does not threaten data integrity. Read-only access should be fast and interactive. A read/modify system will require special host software in order to extract data. Extraction may be either interactive or batch-oriented and may require subsequent translation into a microcomputer format before processing at the microcomputer workstation.

When you are using a read/modify system, you must first determine if a micro uploading of data is workable. In general, micro uploading can work in a corporation, but it requires rigid controls and procedures because of the potential threat to data integrity. One solution is to create intermediate steps in the uploading process that maintain data security and integrity. This can be accomplished by uploading data into a temporary storage area (*dataset*) rather than directly into a mainframe database. The data in temporary storage can then be checked for validity before uploading into the database, thus maintaining the integrity of the mainframe database.

This approach also enables the user or others to access the uploaded dataset for other processing. A dataset from Lotus' 1-2-3 on the micro could be uploaded to the mainframe and accessed by several people. Furthermore, the dataset could be used by mainframe programs if necessary. Overall, uploading to datasets may offer the flexibility of utilizing the data multiple times based on a one-time upload; it may also help to maintain good data integrity and security.

DATA RESPONSIBILITY

Any computer environment needs some type of data administrator. The administrator is responsible for security and overall data integrity. Day-to-day business decisions are based on information from computer systems. It is vital that the information in the system be as accurate as possible. Data processing departments typically control the ownership of and access to computer-based information. Some environments have a custodian of data known as the database administrator (DBA). The DBA's main responsibility is to maintain the overall data integrity of the information stored in databases or files. The DBA may also be in charge of security and related procedures surrounding the authorized access to information.

As the decentralization wave sweeps across the data processing industry, the issues of data ownership, security, accuracy, and administration become even more complex. Because of the explosive growth of microcomputers, the data-responsibility problems are distributed across a broad spectrum of individuals. An important question then is: who is responsible for financial information, once it has been extracted into a microcomputer spreadsheet?

Another related question concerns conflicting versions of the same data. One person may generate reports on the microcomputer and send them to management. At the same time, management also receives reports — based on the same information — from the central mainframe area. Normally, both sets of data have been manipulated and reflect somewhat different conclusions. Which report is accurate?

Thus, there are many issues for a corporation to resolve in the area of data integrity and responsibility. And there are distinct trade-offs between the central DP department and the distributed microcomputer when the issue of data responsibility is raised.

SUMMARY

Micro users will increasingly do much more of their own data retrieval without help from DP personnel, so it is important for them to understand how data is stored. Computer data is stored in structures called databases. Three types of database are in common use: hierarchical, relational, and network.

The relational database is the simplest, using a row-and-column type of organization. The hierarchical is more efficient because it offers shortcut paths to particular information in the database. However, the hierarchical database is more difficult to use. When information from multiple databases may be part of a single report, the shortcut paths of the hierarchical structure are highly beneficial. It's also helpful if these multiple databases can be tied together so that they can be used as a group. When hierarchical databases are tied together in this manner, the structure is called a network database management system.

A database management system (DBMS) is a software program designed to create and manage the database. The individual who is responsible for data integrity and security is called the database administrator (DBA).

Access to the database may be either of two types: read-only (query) or read/modify (extraction). A query is a simple request to read certain data without modifying or even copying it. Extraction, on the other hand, involves reading with the intention of modifying the data. Understanding databases and their structures is a key ingredient in the quest for mainframe-to-micro integration.

5. Data Extraction

GOOD data is invaluable to an organization. Tremendous systems have been built to gather data, along with larger and larger devices in which to store that data. Yet as the amount of stored data has grown, it has created a related problem — how can the data be used efficiently? How do you even begin to sort through the vast accumulations of information to find the data you need?

From your earliest school days, you've learned certain strategies for finding data. You look through indexes to find titles that suggest appropriate material. Then you retrieve these titles (the actual book, article, or report). Usually a considerable amount of additional searching, culling, and distillation of information must follow. Finally, the data is in a form that is usable for actual analysis.

Such physical data searches are seldom feasible today because of the amount of data that must be searched. Fortunately, computers are excellent tools for finding and preparing data for analysis. However, computers still have their limitations. In particular, computers cannot infer, reason, or offer opinions. They will do exactly what they are told to do, no more and no less. Even though a person can use a microcomputer to gather and manipulate data, people must supply the instructions required to make these things happen. This need is immediately obvious when it comes to finding the data.

FINDING THE DATA

Before data can be prepared for use, they must first be located. Doing this often means that a person must define the data explicitly and then tell the computer precisely where to find them. As users of microcomputers frequently discover, data can be temporarily lost, even on a 360KB floppy disk. When the data is stored within a multimegabyte database on the mainframe, finding it may take on a "needle-in-the-haystack" futility.

To find data in a computer database requires some knowledge of how that database is structured. Chapter 4 discussed three common database structures: hierarchical, relational, and network. Relational and network databases provide the easiest method of finding data; the user simply names or gives the parameters of the required information and the database software begins to search. Yet, even in these structures, the user must know that the data exist and exactly how they are stored.

The hierarchical database is much more complex. In addition to the data's existence and structure, the user also must know the path to the data. For example, to retrieve data on a hierarchical database, the major grouping and every minor grouping that encompasses the data must be specified. Because so much information must be provided to the computer before anything can be found, data is often lost in hierarchical database searches. Once again, trained data processing professionals are needed to program searches of hierarchical databases.

PUTTING USERS IN CONTROL

Not only do computers need precise instructions; the instructions themselves must be written in a precise format. Typically, the formats involve cryptic abbreviations and mathematical symbols that are actually a *query*, or programming language specially written for the database. Because using a programming language is a complex skill, people traditionally rely on a programmer. The programmer then writes a *menu* that will allow the user to create requests in the proper format. (A menu presents the user with options in plain English on the computer screen.)

Custom menus have two drawbacks.First, the user cannot enter the database until the menu is programmed. Second, the menu is normally an inflexible tool; if a person wants to access other data, another menu must be programmed.

A new generation of database management software is solving these problems by providing flexible data access screens. People can describe the data that they need in plain English. Any data within the database can be accessed, without the need to first request special programs for the DP department.

EXTRACTING THE DATA

In the mainframe-micro environment, software that allows micro users to access mainframe data is called *data-extraction software*. Figure 5–1 shows the series of processes through which data must pass in the mainframe-micro link. The upper level represents the mainframe data, which was discussed in chapter 4. The next level is data extraction.

Data extraction is not new to data processing; it has been in use virtually since the first computer systems. When data extraction is performed through a terminal, a person selects specific data from a menu of command sequences. The data is extracted and sent to the terminal, either to be listed on a printer or to be scrolled onto the terminal screen. If further analysis is required, it is left to the noncomputerized tools of the analyst — paper and pencil.

The industry is now moving away from the simple mainframe-terminal relationship and into the age of the micro. The mainframe-micro extracting mechanism has many more variables to be considered (see figure 5–2). The micro can be used as a processor, just as the mainframe can. To allow users to benefit from both the mainframe and the micro, it is necessary to bridge the gap between the two machines.

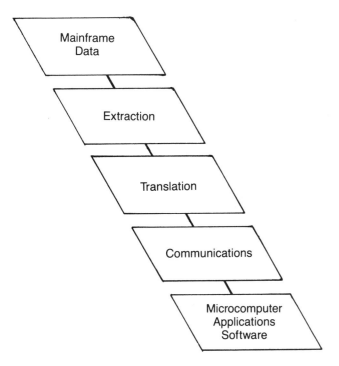

FIGURE 5–1: *The mainframe-micro model illustrates the layers of mainframe-micro integration. The database, with its collection of data, is the first layer of the model. The second layer is the data-extraction process, in which data are removed, consolidated, and formatted in preparation for subsequent processing.*

BRIDGING THE COMPATIBILITY GAP

The goal of mainframe-micro packages is not only to perform the extraction but also to transmit the data to the micro for processing. As can be seen from the mainframe-micro model (figure 5–1), this involves several steps, one of which is making the mainframe data compatible with the micro.

Compatibility is not limited to actual data format. The size of the transferred data file must also be compatible with the micro storage capacity. The amount of data that a person requests could be too large to be stored at a microcomputer. Also, the applications software at the microcomputer may be restricted in the size of file it can handle.

Some mainframe-micro link packages provide the capability to extract data in either detail or summarized records. Summarization means, "Under certain conditions, consolidate the data in a specific manner." Detail means, "Under these conditions,

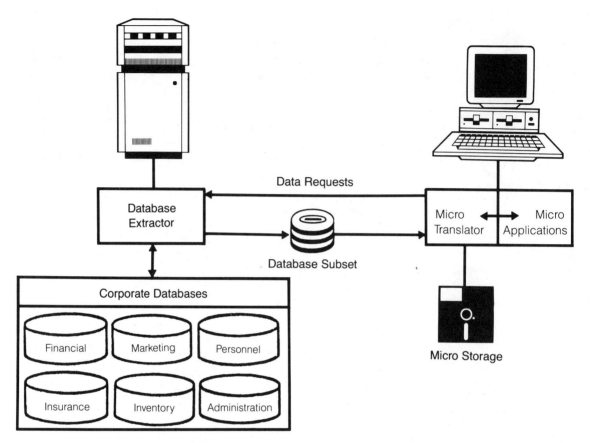

FIGURE 5–2: *Both the mainframe and the micro can be used to process data. After data are extracted, they are held in a temporary location (database subset) until they can be delivered.*

give me everything." Deciding on whether to use detail selection is one of the important choices that users must make. Detail records, or records without summarization, often waste time.

Detail reports require the user to manage a tremendous amount of data. Much of this data may not be pertinent to the analysis. Few jobs are more laborious and unrewarding than going through a report with 100 fields and hundreds of entries, when all that's wanted are one or two fields from a single line. Because of this, selective summarization is usually the preferred reporting method when moving data from mainframe to micro. Summarization provides a concise reporting vehicle.

AN EXAMPLE OF DATA EXTRACTION

In step one of the extraction process a person builds a request. This might include specifying certain data and requesting that it be reported as summarized or detailed. The extractor/report writer might be further instructed as follows: "At this particular field, insert a group break. Every time the department title changes, print a total for the department." Or, "print a total on the X field every time the A field changes." The actual definition of how the data should be extracted may change from person to person.

The importance of selecting or extracting only relevant information can make the difference between an effective or ineffective mainframe-micro relationship. Consider individuals using an extractor in an insurance company's remote office. The central database is kept at the home office, located in a different state. The remote office personnel wish to extract out of the central database only data pertaining to agencies and geographical locations pertinent to the remote office.

The request might be as follows:

1. I want database RO25.
2. I want it for the West (geographic area).
3. I want agents Smith, Jones, Brown.
4. I want the dollar amount of policies sold this year for each agent.
5. When the data is extracted, every time the agent name changes, I want a total of all his policies.

The extractor/report writer will go through the entire database and extract the requested data. If John Smith has sold 20 policies, the extracted data will list all 20 policies. The summarization will come at the last line, saying Smith has sold $1 million worth of policies or some such number. The detail — that is, the names of policy holders, dates of sale, and other information concerning Smith's production — will appear above the total.

SORTING AS A FEATURE

In addition to summarization, another capability that is often valuable in a mainframe-micro data extraction package is *sorting*. Sorting is the process of arranging the data in the order most suited to the task. In creating a report, the sorting feature can be used to format the extracted data into certain columns on the report. Then the columns can be sorted prior to the report being delivered to the micro.

INTERACTIVE OR BATCH EXTRACTION

There are two common ways to use data on a computer: interactively or via scheduled processing (batch processing). Each has its advantages and disadvantages.

Interactive extraction is an on-line process, meaning that if a person requests some data to be extracted, it will be processed and delivered immediately. One problem with interactive extraction is that it can be highly resource-intensive from the standpoint of CPU and communications network load. Interactive extraction requires that the communications connection to the mainframe remain open while the request is processed. If several people are using interactive processing on the mainframe, the process can contribute to a degradation of performance.

For small amounts of data, interactive extraction may be justified. If a person is going to download only 100 or 200 records interactively, the effect is negligible. If 5,000 records are going to be brought down and 30 other people are also trying to download large numbers of records, however, the load may be intolerable. One method of controlling system and network overload is through scheduled, or batch, processing.

Batch extraction can be a resource-conservative method of processing data. A batch job can be processed late at night when the computer is lightly used. Alternatively, people can enter all of their batch requests in the morning, for processing during some other off-time, such as lunch, when interactive use of the system is at a minimum. Because it can be scheduled for optimum times to conflict as little as possible with other system activities, the batch method is especially desirable for large file extraction.

Thus, the size of the data can be a primary factor in determining the method of extraction, whether interactive or batch. A good extraction product should offer the option of either method, just as it should offer sorting and summarization techniques.

Up to this point data extraction has been examined only from a mainframe perspective. The microcomputer offers other possibilities.

EXTRACTION AT THE MICROCOMPUTER

Extraction at the mainframe is usually the preferred method of doing data extraction, because the process is performed at the level where high-speed processors can be utilized. Furthermore, because data is stored at the mainframe, manipulation is easier. This means that only the desired data is transmitted across the communications network.

Micro-based extraction is typically limited to small amounts of data. Micro-based extractors are usually designed to capture data scrolling across the screen. That data is then extracted one screen at a time. Micro-based extractors can be labor-intensive. They may require a person to interact constantly with the software. In many cases, the end-user must confirm a request and press the Enter key before extraction will take place. After this, the next screen of information is displayed for processing.

Because of the potential labor-intensive nature of these processes, micro-based extraction is much slower than mainframe-based extraction. It also can be more prone to error, relying too much on user intervention.

METHODS OF MICRO-BASED EXTRACTION

With mainframe extractors, once the request for data extraction has been made, the process of selection, extraction, summarization, and transmission is performed with little additional user interaction. When data extraction is done at the micro, however, someone usually must be present during the entire process.

Micro-based data extractors are available in two basic types: *snapshot* and *dynamic data capture*. Snapshot extractors require a person to take an entire screen of information at once, which is then written to the microcomputer's storage media. With the snapshot method, all images on the screen will be captured, including needed data, unneeded data, and even garbled characters. Cleaning this up may require more work than is justified from a cost or time viewpoint.

Dynamic data capture is a more powerful means of micro extraction. A person can define a particular area of the screen that will contain the desired data. This method allows unwanted information to be bypassed. Dynamic data capture at the microcomputer is similar to data extraction on a terminal. You request data, and the data will then list across the screen. Normally, a terminal will list a screenful of data and then stop. Using dynamic data capture you can define (referred to as "painting") the area on the screen that you want to extract and save.

Being able to selectively define the area of the screen to be captured can be useful. Consider a mainframe database that contains an employee's first name, last name, street address, city, state, and zip code. You may want a report that uses only the last name and zip code. With micro extractor software, you would paint those fields as they come across the screen the first time. After that the software ignores all the other fields on the screen. As screen after screen of data scroll across the display, the micro will extract information only in the two defined areas.

Both micro-based extractors, snapshot and dynamic data capture, rely heavily on communications response time. If a 1200-baud dial-up line is being used, the data will come onto the screen slowly. Extraction won't take place until the data is painted on the screen. In other words, the extraction process will be just as slow as your communications. Micro-based data extractors should be used only when a limited amount of data is being requested.

In contrast, when extraction is done at the mainframe, communications aren't used until the extraction, summarization, and reporting are completed. When this processing is completed, the data is downloaded. Only the selected data is transmitted, whereas with a micro extractor the entire file is transmitted.

SUMMARY

Modern data-extraction software brings mainframe databases closer to the end-user. General-purpose database menus allow nonprogrammers to access data and avoid the need for DP programming.

Extractors permit the user to select, extract, and download data. Other desirable features to look for in a mainframe-micro extractor are summarization and sorting. These two techniques can help minimize the amount of data transmitted to the micro. Furthermore, communication speed and error checking will be key factors in overall efficiency of the extraction process.

Data can be extracted at the mainframe or at the microcomputer. For small amounts of data, micro-based extractors are adequate. Because micro-based extractors can waste communications resources and require continuous user interaction, however, they should not be used for large file extraction. In that case, a mainframe-based extractor may be preferable. In general, mainframe-based extractors are the preferred method for data extrapolation.

6. Data Translation

IN the mainframe-micro model (see figure 6–1), the third layer is data translation. Translation naturally follows data extraction. One of the difficulties in the mainframe-micro link is that mainframes and micros cannot easily read each other's data. Simply downloading data to a microcomputer is only half the battle. The other half is translating the data so that it's compatible with microcomputer software applications.

Individuals who use microcomputers often have difficulty understanding the issue of compatibility. Their computers and software all work with the same letters and numbers; why can't they talk to one another? In fact, few systems can communicate directly. The reasons for incompatibility are as fundamental as the character sets used on computers. Computers don't understand letters or numbers or any other complex symbols. A computer can understand only binary code, which is a series of 1s and 0s. Binary patterns can be used to represent letters and numbers, and that's how character sets are built. Data on IBM mainframes is written in Extended Binary Coded Decimal Interchange Code (EBCDIC) character sets, whereas data on microcomputers is written in American Standard Code for Information Interchange (ASCII) character sets. For example, the letter A in EBCDIC is 11000001; in ASCII, A is 1000001.

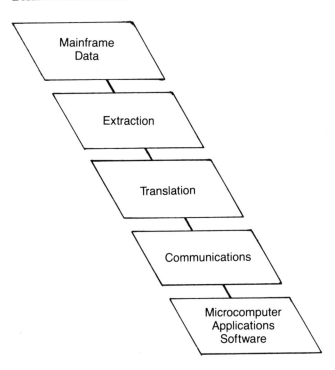

FIGURE 6–1: *After data are extracted, they must be converted into a usable form. This conversion takes place in the translation layer.*

Even when software programs use identical character sets, the data still may not be compatible. Applications software packages are seldom capable of exchanging data, because they use different schemes for arranging information called *formats*. Data in a mainframe VM/CMS file cannot be easily transferred to the mainframe TSO environment. At the micro level, computations and analyses developed on a spreadsheet package usually cannot be merged easily into a text document or even another brand of spreadsheet.

PLANNING FOR FILE COMPATIBILITY

A possible solution to mainframe-micro compatibiliy is to install versions of the same applications software at each end of the link. For example, if the mainframe database management system is available in a microcomputer version, then file compatibility between the two systems is improved. This commonality in software is known as mainframe-micro *integrated software*, and is discussed in depth in chapter 12. Frequently, though, integrated packages may not be available for a specific application. Existing mainframe database programs may have no micro software counterpart. Even when a new mainframe-micro integrated product is available, the cost of converting to a new database environment may be extremely high and unjustifiable.

If a good integrated package is suitable, it may solve the compatibility problem entirely. Integrated database software lets people move information from a mainframe database to a micro with little or no translation or conversion necessary. However, when software other than integrated packages is used, translation becomes a necessary element in a mainframe-micro link.

THE TRANSLATION UTILITY

To move data from a mainframe database down to the micro level requires data extraction. An important component of such a product is a translation utility, which can be based on either a mainframe or a micro. Conversion should be possible in both directions. The translator must be able to translate host data into a proper microcomputer format and to reverse the process.

Mainframe-based Translation

A mainframe-based translation tool usually works in conjunction with a mainframe-based extractor. A mainframe-micro product that offers the capabilities of extracting the data will usually possess an integral feature that performs the translation.

From the end-user's viewpoint, mainframe-based translation is a simple process. Assume that a mainframe-based extractor was used, the extraction process has been completed, and the data have been summarized. The report file is still stored at the mainframe. The next step, before downloading to the micro, is to translate the data into a format suitable for the micro.

At this point, the required micro format must be specified. If data will be taken into dBASE III on the micro, the person using the translator requests that the data be translated into a dBASE III file format. For a mainframe-to-micro translation utility to cover the majority of users, a company should standardize on certain microcomputer software packages whenever possible. When a database extractor and associated translator are selected, they should be chosen with specific micro applications in mind. A mainframe-based translator is of little value if it translates mainframe data into a format that isn't in common use at the micro level. Unfortunately, there are few standard micro file formats. As a result, coordination among individuals in selecting mainframe-micro products is important.

Compatibility is also an issue when new applications software is subsequently selected. A mainframe-based translator routine will usually translate into only a fixed number of formats. For example, it may support 1-2-3, dBASE III, and also SuperCalc formats but not provide translation for that new wonderful software program that just became available. Microcomputer users should be forewarned that new applications software may not be supported by the currently installed translator. In many cases, the micro formats supported by a mainframe-micro translator utility can help foster standards regarding microcomputer software used by a company. If people are aware that only certain micro formats are available, they may be less inclined to purchase every new unsupported product.

Microcomputer-based Translation

A micro-based translator works with files that have been extracted from the mainframe and transmitted to the micro without prior translation. The thrust of a micro-based translator is that it performs the translation after data are moved to the microcomputer floppy or hard disk. The translation may be needed for data that have been pulled down from the mainframe or for data locally stored on the micro from a different application.

In some instances, micro-based translators are used in addition to mainframe translators. An organization may use a mainframe-based translator that is limited to four micro software formats. If additional formats are required, a micro-based translator could be used in conjunction with the mainframe translator. Combining the two would offer greater flexibility in the types of microcomputer software supported. A company simply cannot change mainframe translators every time new micro packages appear. The micro-based translator can serve as a interim solution.

A micro-based translator could allow the user to reformat the 1-2-3 file for a new application format. Data might be extracted from the mainframe database, translated into a 1-2-3 format, and sent to the micro. At that point, the end user may decide to use a software package other than 1-2-3. Translation from one micro format to another is often desirable, for example, when inserting spreadsheet data into a document that is primarily text.

Alternatively, micro-based translators can be used as a primary translation tool. Micro users in such a situation would download data "as is" from the mainframe. They could then use a generic micro-based translation utility package. These generalized software utilities can read a standard file and change its format by asking questions such as, "Do you want the file output in XYZ format? ABC format?" and so forth. Data conversion should be supported at any level, including file, record, and field levels. Furthermore, data conversion or translation may support summarization and sorting.

Several software packages are available that perform data translation or conversion at the micro. All microcomputer users in a company should purchase the same conversion software, whenever possible. Furthermore, careful analysis and testing should be performed on the products.

A problem with micro-based utilities purchased by end users is that they may select poor conversion software. This can result in grossly inaccurate data conversions. Poor conversion software may even cause the loss of data. Thus, data integrity is threatened, and stronger audit trails and text audits are needed. Furthermore, low-level utilities may not be properly maintained by the vendor.

DATA INTEGRITY AND TRANSLATION

Caution is advisable when more than one level of translation is used — for example, when a micro-based translator is used after mainframe-based translation. The more times data is translated or converted from one format to another, the more chances there are of introducing errors or losing data. The data may be accidentally changed through some idiosyncrasy of the software. Thus, the introduction of additional layers of translation poses a threat to data integrity.

When data is moved from one environment to another or from one format to another, every effort should be made to verify that the information is not unintentionally altered. Although it is a functional requirement to move data from one environment to another, data translation is never guaranteed to be error-free. Translation software is normally faithful in its movement of alphanumeric characters, but control codes and nonprinting characters are frequently garbled or lost.

The Escape character, which is normally inserted by pressing the Esc key on a micro, is a frequent cause of translation errors. Most printers accept commands that are a letter or number preceded by the Escape character. In one example, an office found that it was getting an abnormally high number of errors in the documents it received. It was found that the translator was inserting the Escape character in the middle of certain lines of text. When the printer saw the Escape character, it immediately interpreted the next character as part of that Escape sequence; occasionally two or three subsequent characters were included as well. Whatever the printer decided belonged to the Escape sequence was deleted from the report. This kind of problem is especially difficult to detect because the Escape character is a nonprinting character; such mistakes often go unnoticed.

Other times, Escape characters that are intentionally inserted can cause errors. If you were to use a large number, such as 23 million, in the middle of a document, you might want to make the number print out in bold type. To print with bold type, the printer must see an Escape character sequence before and after the word. If the translator does not properly convert the Escape sequence from one format to another, 23 million can easily become 3 million on the final document. It may be hard to explain a loss of $20 million.

INFORMATION TRANSLATION

So far the discussion of translation has focused on software utilities. Translation between the mainframe and the micro is, however, also affected by the user.

Data integrity and translation is a complex problem. To understand it fully requires making a distinction between data and information. Data integrity in translation is more concerned with downloading information than with downloading data. The concept of data is easy to define: data are made up of a series of bits. On the other hand, information involves *where* the data is placed and *how* the data are presented. Also, information is the total content of a document or file; partial losses of content may materially alter the informational value of the message.

When data are moved and converted from one format to another, the user should make certain that the data received represents the same information that was sent. In a host-to-terminal environment, the user's role is minimized: if a financial report is taken from a mainframe, the user first may verify it on the terminal screen. The report is then printed out, perhaps to be distributed at a meeting. Because terminals can only request data, not modify it, the report is probably a true representation of data on the mainframe.

In a mainframe-to-micro environment, on the other hand, the mainframe data can be converted for use in a microcomputer application, but significant data may be omitted in the conversion process. For example, footnotes contained in the original mainframe report might be left out in the micro version. If the user did not fully understand the meaning of the original mainframe report and therefore did not notice a few omissions, the meaning of the report could be totally changed. Micros are often criticized for poor data integrity, but the real problem is often attributable to a lack of awareness of the original content on the part of the user.

IN-HOUSE PROGRAMMING

Another way to convert into PC format and vice versa is to use in-house programming. However, some drawbacks are associated with development of such utilities. First, in-house programming tends to be considerably more expensive than commercial off-the-shelf software. Also, maintenance is an ongoing, often expensive requirement; when a commercial translator is used, the vendor can be expected to provide maintenance at a lower rate than similar in-house support would cost.

When software is written in-house, it is often difficult to obtain the high level of user-friendliness found in today's commercial software packages. Most corporate data processing programmers are used to developing systems software, such as accounts receivable and accounts payable. The people who use these programs are extensively trained for the particular application, and often that application is their primary activity. In these situations, the special programming enhancements designed to aid casual users are often omitted.

Microcomputer users, however, have different needs. Typically they must use many programs. Also, the percentage of total work hours at the micro may be low. Because they plan to spend little time on each application, micro users expect a much friendlier end-user interface than is commonly developed by most mainframe applications.

SUMMARY

Overall, a mainframe-based translator is preferable to a micro-based translator. The mainframe-based translator can be an aid in standardization. Using a mainframe product that translates data into particular formats helps to encourage standards for software at the micro, because there are limited numbers of micro packages that each translator can support. Users will be prone to stick with products that the mainframe-to-micro link supports.

Translators can reside in either the mainframe or the micro. Both types of translators serve the generic need of putting mainframe data into a micrcomputer format or vice versa. It is important that translators not be used blindly. Verify and then re-verify final results to ensure that what you received matches precisely what was sent.

7. Protocols

COMPUTER systems can, and often should, be composed of more than one technology. Sharing technologies helps provide an overall solution that is appropriate to each environment. Considerable flexibility exists in the ways these choices can be implemented.

When a computer signal is sent onto a cable or other medium, it can be received only by a device employing the same rules. These rules are referred to as *protocols*. Protocols are standards developed to permit two devices to communicate. Communications protocols cover every aspect of communication: the type of cable used to carry the signal, the electronic characteristics of the signal, the address/acknowledgment system for messages, and much more. An in-depth discussion of protocols is beyond the technical scope of this book, but understanding the concept of *data transmission* and selecting the best method for a mainframe-micro link requires at least an introduction to some of the more important aspects of communication protocols.

Several kinds of communication protocols exist: physical or interface protocols, data-link control protocols, network-management protocols, and end-to-end data transport protocols.

Each of these protocols has its own function within a network or communication process. The protocols work together to complete a data transmission and reception.

The physical or interface protocol is a so-called low-level protocol. It defines the electrical characteristic and specifies the physical elements that are being connected in the communications system, such as computer-to-computer, computer-to-printer, and so forth. The data-link control protocol, which is also described as low level, controls the functions necessary for point-to-point data transfer. The network management protocol ensures that data is delivered accurately, even in the event of failure in a protocol at a lower level. Finally, the end-to-end data transport protocol establishes and maintains organized transmission between communication devices on the network.

To establish successful communications between two devices, a communications link must implement the physical, data-link control, network-management, and end-to-end data transport protocols. Some additional levels of communications protocols support higher-level services of the communications link.

TYPES OF PROTOCOLS

Two common protocol "classes" are used in the data-transmission process: asynchronous (async), which is sometimes referred to as the start/stop protocol, and synchronous (sync). Async and sync are described as classes because there are many variations of each. To explain the difference between these two classes of protocols, an understanding of some fundamental computer terminology is needed.

A *bit* (contraction of BInary digiT) is the smallest unit of information in the binary system of notation. Binary characters are represented by 1s and 0s. A 1 bit is detected when an electronic impulse is transmitted via a communication path. This is also referred to as the *on condition*. When no electrical impulse is detected in a bit character stream, a 0 bit is assigned to the receiver. This is known as the *off condition.* A series of bits, usually eight, is needed to construct a *byte,* which is defined as a binary element string of eight bits used to represent a character.

Asynchronous transmission is a bit-oriented data-transmission protocol. Each character transmitted is represented by a string of eight bits. A start bit, usually one 0 bit, indicates to the receiver that the next eight bits will construct a single character. After all the character bits, plus the start bit, have been transmitted, the trailing bits, usually two 1 bits or a 1 bit and a 0 bit (10), indicate to the receiver that transmission for that character is complete. This process is repeated until all the characters in the transfer file have been transmitted over the communications path.

In some descriptions, the starting 0 bit is referred to as a space and the trailing 1 bit as a mark, or marks, depending on the design.

The start/stop bit transmission provides a way for the transmitting computer to inform the receiving computer of the significance of the information being received. With start/stop transmission, characters can be transmitted randomly, because each character carries the necessary identification information within itself.

Synchronous transmission is a byte-oriented protocol. Each block of data in a sync transmission is preceded by at least two "sync" or "synchronizing" characters. When the first sync characters are detected, automatic synchronization takes place. The receiver will accept all bits transmitted without interruption. This process remains constant until some other sync characters are detected, indicating that the entire data block has been transferred.

All data transmissions use some type of communication protocol to establish and maintain the connection. If protocol acknowledgment between communicating computers is not established, no communication will occur.

Before any of the popular communications protocols are discussed, some of the necessary physical properties of transmitted information should be examined.

FORMS OF INFORMATION

Information signals are either analog or digital. *Analog* refers to the signal resulting from a physical process, such as the change of air pressure used in analog information signals. Pressure causes the air to vibrate, creating sound frequencies commonly referred to as AM (amplitude modulation) or FM (frequency modulation). As the sound is transmitted over a communication line, the receiver takes it, interprets its frequencies (known as Hertz), and assigns it a binary value of zero or one. This process is called *frequency division multiplexing.*

When the digital form of information signal is used, an electrical signal, representing a numeric quantity or coded symbol, is transmitted over the communication line. Usually the coded symbol is based on either the binary number system or the decimal numbering system.

Thus, for information to be transmitted from one point to another or from one piece of equipment to another piece of equipment, some method of transmitting and receiving must be available. Currently, most information transmissions include the use of electrical impulses or signals. Before the transmission can be made, there must be a physical connection. Usually, coaxial cable, twisted wire, or some other type of electrical conductor is used.

Other forms of information transfer, such as fiber optical data transfer, can be used. In fiber optical transfer, light is used as the information exchange medium between two transmission points. The light is carried via a thin strand of flexible glass fiber. Another transfer method is microwave transmission. Microwave information signals can pass through the air without using physical connection cables. Both the fiber-optical and the microwave data-transmission methods are currently limited to general experimental use. They offer significant advantages in special applications, and their eventual widespread adoption is virtually a certainty. Before they become widespread, however, special protocols to deal with their unique characteristics must be developed.

POPULAR PROTOCOLS AND STANDARDS

Some of the popular protocols and standards used by most tele-communication facilities and on computer networks include the binary synchronous communication protocol (BSC), the synchronous data-link communication protocol (SDLC), and the CCITT X.25 Packet Switching Interface, which is a popular interface standard.

Binary Synchronous Communication Protocol

The binary synchronous communication protocol (BSC or, more commonly, *bisync*) has been used since 1964. It was developed by IBM for high-speed synchronous data transmission. It is the most widely used protocol by independent vendors whose products emulate IBM terminals, such as the 2780 and the 3270. One shortcoming of bisync is that it does not support full-duplex data transmission; it can be used, however, with full-duplex or half-duplex channels. (*Full-duplex* means that simultaneous two-way transmissions are possible; *half-duplex* means that only one-way transmission is possible.)

With the bisync protocol, synchronous techniques are used to transmit blocks of data. Synchronization is achieved by sending a specific bit pattern, called a *sync character*, at the start of transmission. The receiver examines this sequence and adjusts its timing to conform to the transmitter. Data are sent as a string of binary digits in serial form, bit-by-bit. Bisync is a highly flexible protocol. It allows the use of variable block lengths and can be used with either EBCDIC or ASCII code. The bisync protocol can be used to transmit data at medium speeds over voice-grade lines or at high speed over conditioned data-grade lines.

Synchronous Data-Link Control

The bisync transmission protocol is quickly being replaced by IBM's SDLC protocol. The synchronous data-link control protocol (SDLC) is rapidly growing in popularity. Like bisync, it was also developed by IBM to accomplish high-speed data transmission. SDLC is used within SNA (Systems Network Architecture), another IBM product (see chapter 16).

SDLC is a uniform technique for handling and maintaining a

single communication line. For example, in multiple-line environments, several communications lines are connected to a remote concentrator. (A concentrator is a device that takes transmissions from several lines and retransmits them over a single line.) Several regional concentrators feed a central host. This kind of communications environment requires a sophisticated control mechanism, much as that supported by SDLC. Network control is implemented in the software of the concentrators, the host computers' front ends, and the host computer itself. SDLC can be used on each communications link independently.

SDLC, unlike its counterpart bisync, is capable of supporting full-duplex channels as well as full-duplex transmission. It is a bit-oriented protocol for the data-link control of a communication channel. Configurations are either multipoint or point-to-point and may be either switched or nonswitched. SDLC is also capable of supporting half-duplex channels and data transmission. SDLC has facilities for handling error detection and recovery procedures for errors introduced by the communications channel.

CCITT X.25 Packet Switching Interface

The CCITT X.25 protocol is frequently used in wide-area networks, with transmissions carried on leased lines or standard telephone lines. Tymnet is a primary user of X.25 for its public packet-switching networks.

X.25 defines three protocol layers: the physical, link, and network. The physical layer specifies CCITT X.21, a hardware interface that is functionally equivalent to RS–232C, which is common on the majority of computers.

PROTOCOL SELECTION

Your chosen communications protocol can have a direct effect on data integrity, no matter what the distance of the transmission. Asynchronous movement of financial data, spreadsheets, or analyses — critical information — is dangerous, because no error checking is supported in the protocol. The dropping of one or two digits is highly likely in long-distance communications. Such undocumented data loss opens you up to potential disaster.

Even with such problems, the majority of companies will implement asynchronous communications networks because they are lower in cost than synchronous networks. Cost-influenced decisions, however, may be ultimately self-defeating. For example, the company may save $100,000 by installing async communications, but it may lose three times that amount over time as a result of garbled transmissions. Considering the importance of some data transmissions, this is not farfetched. The possible eventual monetary loss and the virtual certainty that data will be lost in async transmissions must be weighed against any possible savings.

Synchronous communications may be more expensive to implement, but you can have the confidence that data integrity is protected, at least at the protocol level. It makes little sense to allow the data to be transmitted in an unprotected manner and then use tight controls, such as database administrators and strict mainframe procedures for protecting your data. The use of protocols that do not support error checking can make the best controls meaningless.

PROTOCOLS AND DATA INTEGRITY

Downloading from mainframe to micro is much more error-prone in an async environment. Usually one way to avoid errors is never to exceed a 1200 baud transmission speed. Although faster modems are available even for normal dial-up telephone lines, it is usually not a good practice to exceed 1200 baud. For long-distance communications, such as those reaching across the country, even 1200 baud transmission with standard async communications can be filled with uncorrected errors. (These problems may be corrected using modems and communications software that add error detection to the standard async protocol.)

SUMMARY

Protocols are the rules and standards associated with data communications. Protocols govern the format, timing, and error control in a message exchange between two communication processes.

Communications protocols can be divided into two basic groups: asynchronous (async), sometimes referred to as the start/stop or the ASCII protocol, and synchronous (sync), which is a byte-oriented protocol. The binary synchronous communication protocol (BSC), the synchronous data-link control protocol (SDLC), and the CCITT X.25 packet-switching interface standard are popular protocols used by today's telecommunication facilities and on microcomputer networks.

The communications protocol is a powerful concept with the potential for standardizing communications. However, no single protocol dominates computer communications. Thus, people will often need to communicate between incompatible protocols. This creates the need for such technology as protocol converters, the subject of chapter 13.

When implementing a mainframe/micro scheme the actual choice of protocol(s) should not be taken lightly. Important areas such as data integrity are directly associated with the choice of a communications protocol.

8. Dial-up Communications

WHEN data must be sent from one device to another, the simplest method of making the connection is with standard telephone lines. This is commonly referred to as *dial-up communications*. Dial-up communications are an almost instant way of connecting remote devices. The connections can span countries and continents, literally anywhere telephone lines have been installed.

THE DIAL-UP MODEM

The components of a dial-up system are the data devices, which act as transmitters and receivers; the telephone lines; and one special piece of equipment, the modem. A modem is a device that makes computer signals compatible with telephone lines.

Computers operate using digital signals, whereas telephone lines use analog signals. (Digital signals carry information using a binary, on/off, code. Analog signals use a more complex continuous, but fluctuating, transmission to carry intelligence.) In a dial-up network, to convert the signals from one form to the other, a modem is used. *Modem* is a contraction of the words *MOdulator/DEModulator.*

The modem takes a digital signal from the computer and converts it to an analog signal that can be transmitted over a telephone line. Once the message reaches its destination, another modem accepts the analog transmission, converts it back to digital, and passes it along to the computer.

FEATURES OF DIAL-UP COMMUNICATIONS

Because it uses readily available telephone lines, the dial-up method of communications is the most popular data-transmission technique. Compared to the preparation and expense necessary to install a cable system for other communication techniques, dial-up is close to an instant communications system — just plug in and communicate, with no additional wiring.

Another often overlooked benefit of the dial-up technique is its portability. Workstations, especially microcomputer workstations, frequently must be moved around an office and between offices. With dial-up communications, it doesn't matter if you move down the hall or across the world; as long as you have access to a modem and a telephone you are in business. With other forms of communications that use cable systems, the cost of moving can often exceed several hundred dollars per move. With dial-up communications, because telephone lines are present in nearly all offices, the cost of a move is usually negligible.

Besides availability, another advantage of dial-up communications is flexibility: dial-up communications can support either asynchronous or synchronous protocols.

Standard Dial-up Asynchronous Communications

The asynchronous dial-up communications method is the dominant standard in data communications. Most computer and peripheral manufacturers include as standard equipment an asynchronous port, which can connect via a modem into dial-up lines. Computer service companies also support async dial-up communications: contacting public database or bulletin board services via a computer usually requires the use of async dial-up connections.

Much of the support for async dial-up communications

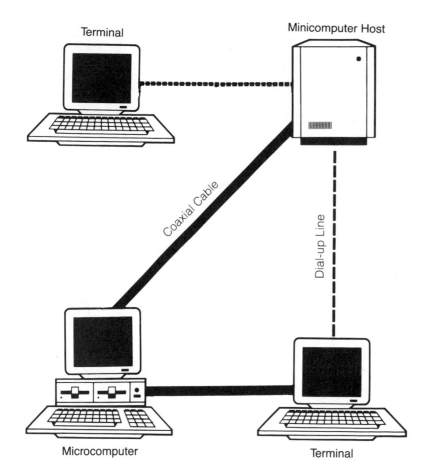

Terminal

Minicomputer Host

Coaxial Cable

Dial-up Line

Microcomputer

Terminal

FIGURE 8–1: *A host computer can simultaneously support a variety of communications techniques, including those using dial-up lines and co-axial cable.*

within major organizations is due to the low cost of such methods. Businesses can save thousands of dollars per workstation by adopting this method, compared to the costs of similar networks using other hardware connections. Async dial-up communications have some significant negative aspects that should be taken into account, however, especially when the intended use is mainframe-micro integration.

Async dial-up communications can be relatively slow, compared to some alternatives. Usually the line speeds are between 300 and 2400 bits per second (bps). The actual throughput speed, which includes line speed and modem processing, can be significantly slower. Faster modems are available, but because of another deficiency of async communications, faster modems may be impractical.

When a signal is driven at a faster rate through a telephone line, it can pick up an increasing amount of noise that produces transmission errors. Standard async communications include no method of error checking and recovery. If two computers are sending information to each other via asynchronous communications and data is lost, the user will not be notified, and the protocol does not initiate retransmission.

When async communications are used across standard phone lines, the same ones that are used for voice communications, 1200 bps is usually a safe speed. Long-distance transmissions should be avoided with async communications, because distance, like speed, can induce errors. Some of these limitations may not apply to general data traffic; in any case, critical data, for the most part, should not be transmitted via async communications. In the absence of an error checking and recovery mechanism, async transmissions are always suspect.

Synchronous Dial-Up Communications

The major alternative to async dial-up communications is the synchronous (sync) dial-up communications method. Sync dial-up communications benefit from the general advantages of dial-up communications: connection over standard telephone lines and connection portability. Like async communications, sync dial-up transmissions require a modem at both sides of each link.

Synchronous dial-up communications are more sophisticated and costly than asynchronous communications. Synchronous modems, for example, are usually more expensive than asynchronous ones. Part of the reason for increased cost is that synchronous modems often deliver higher speeds than async modems, usually in the range of 2400 bps to 9600 bps. Higher speeds are possible using synchronous protocol, because of a built-in error-checking and recovery mechanism. While data is being sent from one computer to another, if a portion of the data is lost, the synchronous protocol will see the error and retransmit the data automatically until it is successfully received.

Error checking and recovery is an essential element in maintaining data integrity throughout an information system. The high data integrity of synchronous dial-up communications is an important advantage.

Two popular synchronous protocols are in use today, the bi-synchronous protocol and the SNA/SDLC protocol. Both protocols were developed by IBM. SNA/SDLC has been identified as the strategic protocol of the future for IBM, and several other large computer manufacturers also endorse SNA.

Although the cost of implementation is higher using synchronous communications, the cost should be weighed against the potential loss of data when using async methods. The loss of even one digit in a transmission can have serious consequences. Where critical data transmissions are concerned, the cost of lost data can make asynchronous communications far more expensive than synchronous.

FILE-TRANSFER ISSUES

Issues of data integrity are particularly important in file transfers between mainframe computers and microcomputers. In many cases, because of the distributed nature of communications, large amounts of data are downloaded to the microcomputer.

The asynchronous communications protocol is by far the most widely used protocol when linking mainframes and microcomputers. As mentioned earlier, the reasons for this are the simple installation and the cost advantages inherent in async techniques. However, little attention is typically given to data integrity. Companies are just beginning to recognize that serious work is being performed on microcomputers. This recognition will force greater attention to the data integrity between mainframe and micro.

In an active data-transfer environment, most people won't take it upon themselves to check the validity of data that has been transmitted to their micros. The most effective means of assuring data integrity, then, is through the use of an automatic procedure entailed within the communications protocol. This relieves some of the burden of the actual end user.

Asynchronous communications offer the advantages of being

inexpensive and easily implemented. If async file transfer is done on a communications network using small files, there may be minimal impact on the communications network. Because of the slow speed of async communications, the actual size of the data being moved up or down the network determines whether async or higher-speed sync communications should be used.

Trade-off and Compromise

One possible option is to use asynchronous transmissions for small transfers and synchronous communications for large data transfer. Standard telephone lines can still be used for both types of transfer. The size of file being transferred can increase with the relative speed enhancement. Synchronous communications, running at speeds between 2400 and 9600 bps, allow large amounts of data to be transferred practically.

The impact of synchronous communications on a communications network, however, must be closely monitored. When you are allowed to transmit at higher rates, there is the tendency to want to transfer much larger or more complex data files. Heavy amounts of data transmission during a specific time can affect overall network performance. The communications load can be monitored and managed in a variety of ways. One strategy is to control the number of dial-up channels. If an organization is concerned about the impact of file transfers, either async or sync, it can limit the number of communications ports at the mainframe. If only ten ports are available, only ten people at a time can transfer files.

Another option for controlling file transfers is to put restrictions on the amount of time that a person can use a given port. For example, end users might be restricted to ten minutes of connect time per session. This opens up the access window to other users and makes the whole user community reconsider the size of transfers.

Of course, the most effective option is to train people to be economical in their use of communications resources (and this applies to all communications strategies). The cardinal rule is this: Don't transmit more data than is necessary. For example, if data is summarized at the mainframe, it can help to minimize the amount of data being transferred to micros.

ENHANCEMENTS TO STANDARD ASYNC COMMUNICATIONS

Synchronous communications offer a way to overcome some of the problems of async transfers, but it is a more expensive approach. Organizations with large installed bases of async devices may not be able to justify the cost of switching to a synchronous network, even though they may want to improve communications integrity. These organizations might well adopt one of the hardware or software products that enhances async communications. A new organization, just starting to install equipment, may have more options.

Async communications' deficiency in error-checking and recovery is not insurmountable. Both hardware and software products are available to enhance async transfers. One such software enhancement for asynchronous communications is BLAST, a product of Communications Research Group. BLAST will be discussed as a good example of such a product, not because it is recommended over others by the authors.

BLAST Asynchronous Communications

BLAST is a family of software and hardware products that enables computers to transfer data using the asychronous protocol. The software performs the file- or data-server functions of BLAST. The hardware component is the BLAST box, an RS–232C asynchronous line adapter that converts normal async output to the full-duplex, 8-bit BLAST protocol.

BLAST is capable of transmitting and receiving binary data files, text files, and commands simultaneously. It can convert a microcomputer into a terminal for on-line sessions and can transfer files to and from a host. BLAST operates on more than 80 different computers: micros, minis, and mainframes.

BLAST adds synchronous protocol type features to async communications. Like the sync protocol, BLAST is a full-duplex, continuous-transmission protocol. It also has some features not found in synchronous protocols, including the ability to automatically reconnect after a disconnection occurs. With BLAST, the synchronous-type features are in software. A network of microcomputers using BLAST can be implemented without special communications circuit boards in each micro and without synchronous modems. BLAST uses asynchronous modems, a dial-up line, and the BLAST components.

BLAST uses a multibuffering technique and takes advantage of the full duplex line to maximize communications capabilities even under adverse line conditions. Full data integrity is assured through the use of a sophisticated error-checking and recovery scheme. The block check is recomputed by the receiving system, and the two values are compared. If the values do not agree, BLAST will retransmit the block. In addition, the BLAST protocol employs several other techniques, such as bit-level data encoding, which make the protocol usable under extraordinarily poor line conditions.

Standard telephone lines, so-called voice-grade lines, are relatively crude media. Transmissions on voice-grade lines can cross through a maze of rough connections and dissimilar environments to reach their destination. These include satellite links, switching systems, and phone lines maintained with greater or lesser care by regional phone companies and long-distance carriers. As a result, virtually every long-distance, point-to-point connection generates line noise. Line noise can be avoided by installing data-grade lines, but the cost may not be justifiable. In many cases, companies choose to use their standard voice-grade lines for async transmission.

A common practice in long-distance data transmission is to set systems up to transmit messages every night. Often, however, when the operators return to work in the morning, the system is dead. Usually, the system encountered excessive noise on the line; when noise reaches the level at which modems lose the carrier, then the systems disconnect. BLAST is programmed to accept short disruptions in service. When it runs into noise, it will initiate a time-out and then redial and retransmit information.

When a block of data is transmitted with standard asynchronous transmission, it moves across a particular channel. The receiving computer sends back an acknowledgment block that says it has received the block. BLAST sends blocks in a stream

in both directions simultaneously (full duplex). The blocks don't have to be received to be acknowledged, because they do not share the same channel.

In other words, a computer in Baltimore might be sending block number 86. The receiving computer in New Orleans can come back on the other channel and say, "Wait a minute; I just detected an error in block number 32. Send it again." The transmitting computer automatically — without user intervention — immediately retransmits block number 32. By the time the other computer receives block 32, the transmitting computer, which has resumed normal transmission, might be on block number 150. The transmitting computer never had to slow down. This is an improvement over even synchronous protocols, such as SDLC and HDLC. When an error is detected on a sync transmission, the transmitting computer must retransmit every block that followed the bad block.

To use BLAST from a microcomputer workstation, the micro user loads BLAST, enters terminal-emulation mode, and then instructs BLAST to dial into a computer that is equipped with a BLAST box. All communications from the micro using BLAST would interact with the BLAST box at the receiving computer. This black box works much as a protocol converter does.

For file transfers, the BLAST host file-server program is brought up under the mainframe environment. At the same time, the user enters BLAST file-transfer mode on the micro. Files can then be downloaded or uploaded between the host and the microcomputer.

SUMMARY

Synchronous communications provide full error checking and recovery and allow transmissions to be made at higher speeds. Such communications provide a practical way of transferring a file of any size file. Even though it is more expensive, the improved data integrity and efficiency often outweigh the higher cost.

The computing world, in general, is moving more toward the use of synchronous communications as a standard. Synchronous protocols, such as IBM's SNA/SDLC, will probably be used on most computers in the future. Concern about data integrity is pushing this trend. This is largely a result of increased use of information transfer. Before the advent of distributed computing, everything was kept in one spot and most communications were inquiries. With file transfers becoming more common, the integrity of the data becomes a serious issue.

Speed, whether from a synchronous system or an enhanced async one, is important. End users should be able to communicate at the highest speed possible. The faster you get information, the faster you can make decisions based on that information.

For many companies, the transition from asynchronous to synchronous communications will occur slowly. Because of the large installed bases of asynchronous equipment, the relatively low cost of implementing such systems, and conversion-cost considerations, asynchronous communications will continue to be utilized.

The lack of error checking and recovery using asynchronous communications should not be taken lightly. Enhancing async networks via software improvements, such as BLAST, or hardware, such as protocol converters, will be more appropriate for many organizations in the short run. Long-term strategies, in most cases, should move in the direction of synchronous communications, such as SNA/SDLC.

9. 3270 Emulation: The On-Line Approach

IN the early 1970s, IBM introduced a new family of communications devices called the 3270 series. The 3270 workstations offer many improvements over the standard terminal, including a greatly improved display and better cursor control. The bisynchronous communications protocol used with 3270 devices provides high-speed communications in the range of 4800 bps to 19.2 bps with full error-checking capabilities.

Since its introduction, the 3270 series has been widely adopted as a method of accessing IBM mainframes. The installed base of 3270 workstations and associated cabling is enormous. Many companies have a large investment in 3270 equipment. These companies have developed large data libraries with mainframe software packages that work only with 3270-type communications equipment. Because of the software and the investment in terminals, printers, cabling, and communications gear, the 3270 series is deeply entrenched.

As microcomputers are integrated into the mainframe system, companies must decide how to integrate these new intelligent workstations into the installed base of 3270 equipment. Should micros functionally replace all of the 3270 terminals? Is a mixture of terminals and micros workable? Can micros physically attach to a 3270 network or must additional money be spent in modifying the communications network?

REPLACING THE TERMINAL

The standard configuration of the bisynchronous 3270 network calls for a 3270-type terminal, which is connected to a control unit via coaxial cable. The control unit is connected to a front-end communications processor, which is attached to a mainframe computer. Several controllers, with their clusters of terminals, can be attached to one mainframe front-end communications processor. Figure 9–1 illustrates a typical 3270 installation.

The tremendous demand for the microcomputer, as well as for 3270 communications, has resulted in the development of 3270 emulation packages for microcomputers. These packages consist of a circuit board that plugs into the microcomputer expansion bus and emulation software that runs on the micro. With the package installed, the microcomputer can emulate, or function as, a full-featured 3270 terminal. Bisynchronous communications between the micro and the IBM host computer can now take place at high speed through the coaxial cable. At the same time, micros can tie into the existing base of 3270 communications equipment.

Connecting the microcomputer to the 3270 via the emulation cards is the same as connecting a terminal to a 3274 controller. A coaxial cable is run from the controller and attached directly to the emulator card in the microcomputer. Once the software is loaded, the micro becomes, effectively, a 3270 terminal. No other physical change is needed. No changes on the host computer, the controllers, or the cabling are required.

At this point, the dumb terminal environment has been replaced with an intelligent workstation. This micro workstation becomes an intelligent 3270 communications terminal and a microcomputer, all in one box. The user has the capability of switching, or *hot-keying*, between a 3270 session with the host and a microcomputer session.

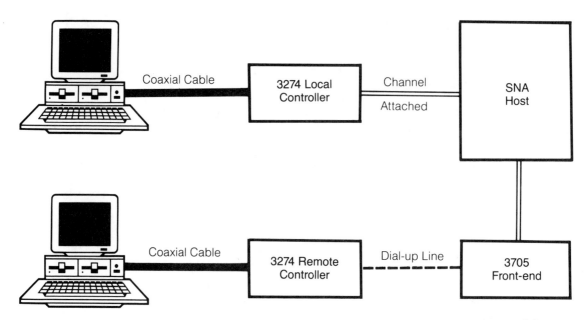

FIGURE 9–1: *A host computer that supports 3270 communications can connect workstations either locally or remotely via communications controllers. A microcomputer attaches to a controller through a 3270-emulation circuit card.*

The microcomputer has another advantage — a reduction in downtime. Mainframe computers can be off-line, or inoperative, as much as 20 percent of the time. Moreover, downtime often occurs during periods of normally high use, which is costly in terms of productivity, because employees must wait for their data. Intelligent workstations overcome this problem by allowing file transfers and local storage. If the mainframe goes down, people often can use their microcomputers in stand-alone mode. With some contingency planning, downtime can be virtually eliminated.

MIGRATING FROM TERMINALS TO MICROS

The transition from a 3270 terminal to a microcomputer emulating a 3270 terminal has been one of the smoothest transitions in computer history. Most transitions in the computer field have required reprogramming of a mainframe and other major modifications. The move to 3270-emulating micros requires no modification other than the switching of the workstations themselves.

The biggest problem in changing from terminals to micro-computers is the keyboard. The keyboards on most microcom-puters are different from those on 3270s. It may take a while for a person who is familiar with the standard 3270 keyboard to get used to the micro keyboard. The transition period will be neg-ligible if the software used on the 3270 system requires minimal typing; however, for a data entry person, the transition period may be lengthy.

The actual physical connection of an emulator-equipped mi-cro to the 3270 network presents little difficulty. Because the emulator is sufficiently plug-compatible, the central data pro-cessing department never needs to get involved.

This high level of compatibility can create its own problem, however. Someone with a 3270 terminal could buy a micro with an emulator and hook it up, and no one would ever need to know that the change was made. One of the concerns of DP depart-ments is that people will install 3270-emulating micros without notifying the DP department and will then start performing file transfers. End users are usually unaware of the impact that file transfers may present.

FILE TRANSFERS VIA EMULATORS

The ability to transfer files is an important feature of the micro, but it can be a potentially serious security and data integrity threat if not handled properly. (The topics of security and data integrity are discussed in several places throughout this book.)

Another, less obvious, problem is caused by the data-process-ing power of the microcomputer. A 3270 network is normally configured for terminals. It is designed to communicate data in 44 to 100 display lines to and from a terminal. An IBM 3274 control unit and associated communications gear has also been designed principally to support terminal-to-host communications.

Terminal-to-host communications are different from micro-to-host communications when file transfer is used. Using file transfer from 3270-emulating microcomputers, you have the capability of sending thousands, even millions of bytes of information to and from a host computer. This increased load on the network can cause real problems across a network: when micro users start transferring files through a common controller, terminal users may experience serious response-time difficulties.

CONTROLLING THE IMPACT

A company has several alternatives for controlling the impact of micros equipped with 3270 emulators. The communications plan could be designed so that a person with a microcomputer could use either 3270 communications or dial-up communications. A person needing to transmit a small file of 40 to 45KB could use dial-up communications when accessing the host. To transmit larger files using higher-speed communications lines, the user could use either the 3270 network or remote job entry. (Remote job entry, or RJE, communications are discussed in chapter 10.)

Ways must be found to combat degradation across the communications network once microcomputers are allowed to conduct massive file transfers. In some installations, additional controllers are installed to spread the data transfer load.

Another method of increasing the throughput of the communication network is to use higher-speed communications lines. The typical speed used to communicate between a 3274 controller and the mainframe is between 4800 and 9600 bps. This range of speed has sufficed for a number of years. With the increased data demands of microcomputers, however, a higher speed than 9600 bps may be needed to maintain a satisfactory communications throughput in the system.

The use of 56 Kbps communication lines will help to offset microcomputer file transfer in many cases. A communications speed of 56 Kbps is approximately six times faster than 9600 bps communications. The faster speed can alleviate the bottleneck associated with microcomputer file transfer.

The conventional controller, an IBM 3274 Cluster Controller, will still be a bottleneck to some extent, however. In the future, the 3274 controllers will be replaced or upgraded with more intelligent, faster controllers. These controllers will be able to process millions of bits of data per second, in contrast to the thousands of bits per second currently processed by most controllers. These higher-speed processors are necessary to handle the high data traffic demands of the future.

In some cases, a minicomputer can be used as a controller. With its faster and more intelligent processing, the mini can outperform a traditional controller. Whether the products are called minicomputers or controllers, the 3274 controller will eventually be replaced by more full-function systems.

Besides providing increased speeds for distributed file transfer, intelligent controllers have the capability of supporting such facilities as dial-up communications and remote job entry. These, in turn, will help to spread and even the load of file transfer across the network.

MULTIPLE 3270 SESSIONS

A recent addition to 3270 capabilities is the ability to have more than one 3270 connection, or session, in progress at the same time. For example, a user might interrogate a mainframe database in one session, compare that information with the another database in a second session, and use the data in an analysis package in a third session. All of these sessions could be displayed simultaneously on the microcomputer screen, each session given an area of the screen, a process called *windowing*. IBM has adopted this technique in its 3270-PC and 3270-PC/GX micro product line.

Although the need for multiple sessions is unusual — normally sessions could be run sequentially with little inconvenience — it may exist. For example, a job that requires extensive data inquiry, such as that of a purchasing department, which handles calls from people who want to know the status of some ordered piece of equipment. In this case, the purchasing clerk must enter a database, type in a purchase order number, and look at a screen of information related to that order. Incoming shipments, stored on another database, must be checked to see if that order has been received. Accounts payable might be searched to see if the order has already been paid for. In this situation, the clerk might need to check three or four databases just to answer the customer's one question.

Databases can be searched sequentially, but response time is slowed while each database is entered, searched, and exited. Here the ability to open multiple sessions simultaneously would be a distinct advantage.

Although the power of having several things going at once is appealing, it is seldom practical. The manager must be cautious of providing one person with multiple session capability. That person can create as great a load on the mainframe, in terms of sessions, as multiple users; for instance, a user who opens four simultaneous sessions on the mainframe creates the same mainframe load as four individual users.

Furthermore, one port on the controller must be dedicated to the workstation for each possible mainframe session. If the workstation can open four sessions simultaneously, that workstation must be given four communications ports on the controller. On a controller that has 32 ports, such as an IBM 3274, a maximum of eight people can be supported if each has four-session capability. If the IBM SNA/SDLC protocol is used, more sessions can be supported on a single controller.

Moving up the communications network, the problem snowballs. With people now tying up more communications ports on the controllers, additional controllers will have to be purchased. This, in turn, will necessitate additional ports on the host front-end processor.

Management is the key to an effective use of resources. A finite number of ports are available at the host. The job at each workstation must be carefully analyzed before multiple windows are authorized. It may be more cost-effective to require the person to open sessions sequentially, even though productivity may decrease somewhat.

Multiple-session workstations, thus, should not be purchased in the same manner that microcomputers are purchased. The proposed use should be carefully scrutinized before purchase is authorized.

WHO NEEDS A MICRO IN THE 3270 ENVIRONMENT?

Today, companies are under tremendous pressure from users to replace their standard terminals with microcomputers. People in large companies want not only the communications to the host computer via 3270 but also the availability of the microcomputer and its associated software. Whether or not the change is beneficial to the company depends upon the requirements of the particular job.

A microcomputer with 3270 terminal capability is ideal for the person who does multiple functions. For example, financial analysts must often access host-computer information, such as the financial database on the mainframe, and interact with it. They must then take that data and analyze it at the local level. Typically this analysis is of a type that the mainframe system cannot perform.

Such an analyst takes the data from the mainframe and has it printed out on a mainframe printer. The analyst then takes that report and lifts the numbers from the printed hardcopy in order to do analysis at the micro. This means that first someone enters the data on the mainframe, then someone prints it out. Finally, someone either re-enters the data into a computer or does pencil-and-paper calculation and types the report.

The advantage of such an analyst having a microcomputer with a 3270 emulator is that after the data is examined on the mainframe, it could be downloaded directly to the microcomputer. In this way, a direct computer-to-computer transfer of information is possible, and data need not be re-entered.

NOT TO USE A MICRO

Companies should not go out and automatically replace all of their terminals with microcomputers. End-user requirements should be the dictating force. Though the cost of 3270 terminals and emulator-equipped micros is approximately the same, there are some valid reasons not to switch to microcomputers.

First, if there is an installed base of 3270s, the microcomputer purchased as a replacement represents an additional cost, not an alternative cost. The cost might be justifiable for a multifaceted job in which a person must use a host and also do local processing, but if 90 percent of a person's activity is data entry into a mainframe and 10 percent is local processing with a micro, replacing terminals with micros may be unwarranted.

Another reason to question the installation of micros as 3270 workstations relates to security. A 3270-type workstation is a secure workstation. A financial database can be designed so that information on the screen can be used in a restricted manner. Authorized users can see the data on the screen, and they might be able to answer questions as part of the program, but they cannot extract data from the screen, put it on a piece of paper, and walk away with it. The data is on the mainframe. The only way to get to that data is through the terminal, and the terminal is protected by passwords and other security mechanisms. The terminal is a look-only, read-only device.

With the microcomputer, a user has a tool that can extract the data from the screen. Letting people take mainframe data and put it into a financial modeling package on the micro may not be desirable. Security is a problem that is often overlooked.

DIAL-UP LINES OR COAXIAL CABLE

The 3270 series is based on the Binary Synchronous Communications (bisync) protocol, which supports a wide variety of media, including both dial-up lines and coaxial cable (see chapter 7). Although 3270 devices can be attached to dial-up lines, the typical choice is coaxial cable.

Companies usually attach 3270 terminals to coaxial cables even in a remote site, where the remote-to-central link might be a dial-up connection. From remote sites, the controller-to-mainframe connection may be implemented with dial-up lines. From the controller down to individual workstations, coaxial cable is normally used.

Many companies decide, for security reasons, not to use dial-up lines for 3270s. The 3270 is considered a secure terminal, and companies don't want people to have dial-up access to what is considered a secure system. In a dial-up system, a person sitting at his micro at home would be able to access any data on the system. Even though security measures are implemented to prevent unauthorized access, the dial-up channel threatens security by providing a ready means to attack the system. If the system requires security, dial-up connections are usually prohibited.

SUMMARY

The 3270 communications network is one of the primary communications networks used in businesses today. The cabling and investment required by the 3270 network is such that many companies cannot afford to disband or remove this communications vehicle. To integrate into the mainframe computing system, the microcomputer must fit into the 3270 network. The advent of 3270 emulation boards makes the migration from terminal to micro an easy one.

Most companies, in order to upgrade their communications facilities to accommodate microcomputers, will look for ways to improve the 3270 network — not to replace it. Improvement may come through such innovations as higher-speed modems and intelligent controllers, higher-speed links between computers, and the availabilty of newer and more efficient protocols.

One such protocol might be IBM's SNA/SDLC protocol, which can be used in a 3270 network without requiring the replacement of much hardware. These innovations will help to offset some of the data-transaction and data-movement loads throughout the 3270 communications network.

10. Remote Job Entry: Batch Transfers

REMOTE job entry (RJE) is a communications method that has been used for many years. RJE operates in a batch mode, instead of interactively as most terminal protocols operate. *Batch mode,* here, refers to a practice in which a large amount of data is processed in one environment and then transmitted as a single unit to another environment. RJE is used for high-speed data transfer between computers, either mainframe to mainframe or mainframe to minicomputer. In some large companies that operate a mainframe in a central site along with distributed minicomputers, RJE is used to move data between these systems.

RJE was designed primarily to handle large volumes of data transmission in nonpeak hours. The batch nature of RJE provides a vehicle to automatically move information between systems. Automatic processing, via RJE, means that at a predetermined time one computer will automatically start transmitting data to another RJE system.

When RJE was first implemented, it dealt with computers that used 80-column cards. Although the punch-card technology is seldom used today, the restriction of 80-character records often remains for uploading data. New micro RJE products are being developed that eliminate this restriction; better products of this type can handle records that are longer than 80 characters, using record-blocking or some other technique.

RJE COMMUNICATIONS

RJE uses the synchronous communication protocol. Because RJE is synchronous, full error checking and recovery are provided within the protocol itself. Dial-up lines are the normal media for RJE. As with other dial-up protocols, RJE transmissions require a modem, in this case a synchronous modem. The modems can be as slow as 300 bps, although high-speed modems that operate from 2400 bps to 9600 bps are more commonly used.

RJE AT THE MICROCOMPUTER

RJE is currently finding use in uploading and downloading files to distributed microcomputer workstations. In some cases, transmission through asynchronous dial-up lines or bisynchronous coaxial cable may accommodate most file-transfer needs between mainframe and micro. Recently, however, the volume of data transfers and the desired higher speed has brought RJE into the forefront as a primary method of file transfer.

The use of RJE at the microcomputer requires a combination of hardware and software (see figure 10–1). The hardware needed includes a synchronous card, which plugs into the micro, and a synchronous modem (usually 2400 bps to 9600 bps). RJE software, which manages the hardware, allows the microcomputer to emulate either 2780, 3780, or HASP RJE protocols. The actual emulation selected by the micro user depends upon which of the protocols (2780, 3780, or HASP) is supported at the mainframe computer. Once the required hardware and software is in place, the microcomputer becomes a full-function RJE station.

RJE capabilities at the microcomputer can be expensive. The combination of hardware and software will average between $1,500 and $2,500 per micro, not including the microcomputer itself, of course. Because users may not need to use RJE continuously to transmit data, the RJE capabilities of a micro should be shared whenever possible. The sharing may be accomplished

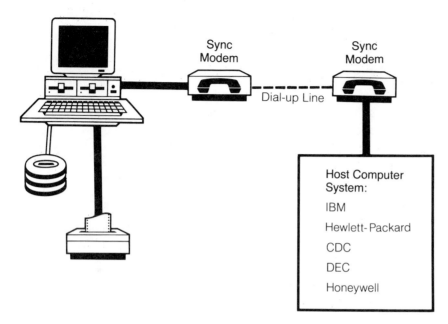

FIGURE 10–1: *RJE communications use a batch process that can be accomplished through the use of 3780 or HASP protocols. Both approaches involve the use of a host computer and synchronous modems.*

in a variety of ways, including through a local area network or by strategically locating the micro for access by others.

MICRO 3780 VERSUS HASP RJE EMULATION

The two most popular RJE emulation approaches for microcomputers are the 3780 and HASP (Houston Automatic Spooling Program) methods. Each approach to high-speed batch file transfer has its own unique qualities along with some characteristics that are common to all RJE.

3780 RJE

The 3780 RJE approach, used extensively to transmit information between mainframes and minicomputers, is now available at the micro level. With 3780 emulation at the microcomputer, you can transfer and receive large amounts of data from any other RJE-equipped computer. The 3780-equipped micro can submit what are called *jobs* or *requests* to another RJE system. These systems can be mainframes, minicomputers, or other microcomputers using RJE. The jobs are submitted and processed by the receiving computer at specified times through *job scheduling*. Such scheduling allows requests for data to be processed during periods when the communications network is lightly used, thereby conserving a host computer's resources.

The scheduling process has another aspect known as *priority sequencing*. Each job that has been submitted can be assigned a number or letter. The letter or number represents a level of priority for processing. Using priority sequencing, more critical jobs, such as accounts payable, can be processed before other jobs. Priorities are yet another means of utilizing computer resources more efficiently.

3780 FILE TRANSFER   RJE supports the uploading of data in 80-character records. As was mentioned earlier, the 80-character limit is based on the old 80-column punch-card technology. Before on-line terminals came into wide use, most data was entered as a batch job on cards with information recorded as small holes punched into the card. Today, a floppy disk can replace the punch cards as the input medium. A typical microcomputer can store approximately 360,000 characters per disk; one disk is equivalent to 4,500 punched cards. Obviously, disks offer a tremendous advantage.

With a microcomputer emulating a 3780 RJE station, you can upload information to an RJE system directly from the micro floppy or hard disk. Because RJE supports high-speed, full-error-checked transmission, large amounts of data can be transferred from the microcomputer.

A 3780-equipped micro also can receive information downloaded from another RJE station. The download process usually offers additional capabilities, such as downloading to a printer, a floppy disk or hard disk, and a plotter. In addition, most 3780-emulation products support downloading of, for example, 132-character records, permitting a 132-column printer to be used during an RJE session. The 132 columns might be used to bring down larger files to be used in microcomputer software programs. However, the 80-character restriction still applies to uploading with most RJE products.

The capabilities of all 3780 emulation products are similar. Common features include such things as unattended operation, prescheduled processing, print and disk spooling, high-speed communications, error checking and recovery, and compression and decompression of data during file transfer. These features are provided in the software. The needed hardware usually includes a high-speed modem, a synchronous card to plug into the micro, and an RS-232-C cable.

HASP Remote Job Entry

HASP is another RJE batch transmission method used on mainframes, minicomputers, and now microcomputers. The HASP protocol grew out of the 2780 and 3780 RJE approaches. Although not as widely known as 3780, HASP offers some powerful advantages.

All of the basic features supported by 3780 are available through HASP, including batch file transfer, high-speed communications, and full error checking and recovery. The modem, card, and cabling are exactly the same in most cases. The real advantage appear in the HASP software protocol design. HASP is more efficient than 3780 and offers greater flexibility in data transmission.

The improved features of the HASP protocol over those of the 3780 protocol are well illustrated by a HASP product called BARR/HASP, by Barr Systems, Inc. BARR/HASP supports a concept known as *interleaving and multileaving*, which allows a microcomputer to transmit and receive data simultaneously. You can receive data from an RJE system and transfer it to a micro printer while simultaneously sending data back to the RJE system. BARR/HASP will also support up to seven printers, either parallel or serial. These printers are supported at speeds in excess of 1,600 lines per minute.

HASP FILE TRANSFER   HASP file transfer is also faster than that of the 3780 protocol. HASP file transfer is optimized in a variety of ways, including buffering and compression/decompression. The compression technique does not transmit duplicate characters or blank spaces in a file. This improves the transfer rate immensely. Once the data is received by another HASP system, the file is expanded, or decompressed, into its original form.

SUMMARY

3780 and HASP cannot be used interchangeably. Companies should choose one or the other. One of the primary benefits of RJE is that it is a mature and well-tested technology that has been in use for many years. This powerful means of file transfer has been made available at the microcomputer level, allowing the micro to be used as a full-function RJE station. RJE supports file transfer of small to large files. Full error checking and recovery is supported through the synchronous protocol. RJE provides a vehicle to control the impact of file transfer through scheduled batch processing.

The controllable load aspect is an important characteristic of RJE. With the influx of microcomputers needing to communicate data to other systems, a method of controlling the impact of file transfer will be critical to many companies. RJE provides such a vehicle. The impact of file transfer between mainframes micros will be felt by many companies. RJE can play a major role in easing the pains of integration.

Although RJE is a good file-transfer alternative for file transfer between mainframe and micro, it has some limitations. First, RJE is a batch file-transfer vehicle only; no interactive terminal emulation is available through RJE. As such, RJE should not be viewed as a replacement for a dial-up terminal-emulation program or a coaxial-attached 3278 emulation board. Rather, it should be viewed as a complementary file-transfer alternative. Very large files are usually more appropriately transmitted via RJE rather than via straight dial-up lines or 3270 coaxial cables.

Finally, the differences between the 3780 emulation and the HASP approaches should be kept in mind. In general, the HASP protocol is more efficient than the 3780 protocol. The HASP method can address multiple devices simultaneously, whereas the 3780 approach is a single-device-operating protocol. Both the 3780 and the HASP protocols provide efficient file-transfer alternatives. When choosing between the two, bear in mind that the receiving RJE system must use the same protocol. For instance, if your mainframe RJE addresses are installed according to 3780 logic, then micros in the same environment must also use the 3780 protocol.

11. Analysis of Link Philosophies

THE previous chapters were designed to provide the background or foundation necessary to evaluate mainframe-to-micro link alternatives. This chapter will focus on three software link alternatives. Several hardware alternatives are also available to connect mainframes and microcomputers; for the purpose of clarity, hardware alternatives will be discussed in later chapters.

Data processing departments can use several methods to move data between mainframes and micros. Whether the process is called *file transfer, data transfer,* or *downloading/uploading,* the object is the same: information interchange between computer systems. Approaches to this information interchange can be divided into three categories; terminal emulation, virtual host storage, and data extraction. The capabilities and implementation impact of each of these approaches will be discussed below. In addition, some specific products that illustrate each link philosophy are mentioned.

TERMINAL EMULATION

The simplest method for interconnecting mainframes and micros is through terminal emulation. Mainframes and minicomputers were designed in a host-to-terminal topology, and every mainframe and minicomputer on the market today supports at least one type of terminal.

These terminals are used as simple input and output devices. In essence, input is through a keyboard and the output is received on the terminal screen. With the terminal receiving increased pressure from the microcomputer as the universal workstation, the problem now is how to connect the microcomputer to the existing mainframe computer network.

Using a combination of hardware and software, the microcomputer can be made to emulate (function as) a terminal. In fact, the micro can emulate a variety of terminals, including an IBM 3101, DEC VT-100, HP 2624, and many others. Besides these dial-up terminals, the micro can emulate terminals attached by coaxial cable, such as the IBM 3278 and 3279.

The important thing to remember is that when it is performing this emulation, the micro appears to the mainframe as just another terminal. No special modifications must be made to accommodate a terminal-emulating micro in a mainframe environment.

Each of the various terminal-emulation approaches has its own characteristics and considerations. The following is an examination how each approach provides the mainframe-micro link.

Dial-up Terminal Emulation

Dial-up terminal emulation at the micro involves a combination of hardware and software. The hardware consists of a modem, a serial port on the computer, and an RS-232-C cable. The software, which resides on a disk, contains the actual terminal-emulation program. This program transforms the micro into a full-function terminal.

For the microcomputer to successfully communicate with another system as a terminal, certain telecommunication parameters must be supplied to the microcomputer emulation program. Once these parameters have been installed, the micro can communicate with the host computer or another micro.

The parameters that must be specified usually include baud rate, stop bits, parity, emulation mode, and phone numbers. The micro parameters must match the parameters of the system with which you intend to communicate. For instance, if the host computer is configured for even parity, the microcomputer emulation program must also be set for even parity. Another important parameter is modem speed or baud rate. If a host computer is equipped with 1200-baud modems, a 2400-baud modem at the microcomputer will be useless. If the micro's transmission speed is at a different rate, the mainframe will disallow the connection.

Making the Connection

Because of recent technological improvements in hardware and software, the connection of a terminal-emulating micro is simple. Assuming the hardware systems are compatible and properly connected, you merely load the emulation software in the micro and tell the program to call another computer. The majority of modems on the market today have a feature known as an *autocall* or *autodial* mechanism, which allows the modem to dial the number automatically.

Once the emulation program calls the desired host and the connection is made, the micro functions exactly as a terminal does. The same commands used on a terminal will operate on the micro. The one major difference between a terminal and a terminal-emulating micro is the keyboard. Unfortunately, because there is no universal keyboard design or layout, the microcomputer keyboard and the terminal keyboard will probably be somewhat different.

Dial-up Data Interchange

One of the major benefits of using a terminal-emulating microcomputer is the availability of data interchange or file transfer with a host system. A tremendous number of companies are replacing terminals with micros. The major reasons are to provide terminal access to a host computer and to move or exchange data between the two environments. Most terminal-emulation programs provide a means of both receiving and sending information between the micro and the host computer.

Two methods are commonly used for receiving the data that is exchanged. One is known as *snapshot processing*; the other is called *data capture.* Each approach to dial-up data interchange offers certain advantages and disadvantages.

SNAPSHOT PROCESSING Snapshot processing requires that information first be brought onto the micro screen. Once the desired information is displayed on the screen, a combination of keys is pressed, which causes the emulation software to copy the exact image of the screen onto a microcomputer storage media (floppy or hard disk).

The snapshot approach captures all information on the screen, whether it is needed or not. This means that any symbols, graphics, headers, etc. are saved along with the desired information. Such extraneous material must be removed manually using an editor or word-processing program.

In some cases a quick snapshot of displayed information is useful. For the most part, the snapshot technique is designed to process small amounts of data. Remember that this approach deals with one screen at a time. Because the information is brought up screen by screen, and a combination of keys must be pressed to save each screen, the snapshot technique is considered labor-intensive. Moving large amounts of data to the micro via this approach may not be practical.

DATA CAPTURE The data-capture approach to extracting information is similar to that of snapshot processing. The needed information must still be brought onto the micro screen prior to being stored at the micro. The difference is that before the information is displayed on the screen, you can specify to the emulation software that all information displayed on the screen should be saved at the micro. Once the emulation software is made aware of this, the micro is in *capture mode.* As the micro receives data from the host computer, the information appearing on the screen is saved. Whenever you wish, you can tell the emulation software to stop capturing data. Everything up to that point will be saved at the micro. Crosstalk, by Microstuf, is a popular microcomputer communications package that uses this technique.

A second approach, known as *dynamic data capture,* goes a couple of steps beyond simple data capture. For instance, you can tell the emulation software to capture only selective portions of the information being displayed. This means, for instance, that you can request that only columns 3, 8, and 10 be saved. Some dynamic-data-capture programs support a technique known as *simulated enter key*. This technique allows the microcomputer emulation program to send an Enter key command automatically, after a specified number of lines of information have been displayed.

With such advanced features, dynamic data capture offers some useful advantages over standard data capture. For example, the simulated Enter key removes the requirement that a person be present to interact with the software constantly; this aids tremendously in overall efficiency of the process.

Uploading Using Terminal Emulation

The uploading process, or the moving of information from micro to host, is much different from the downloading approaches (snapshot and data capture). The majority of the microcomputer dial-up terminal-emulation programs use the facilities of a host editor to move the data from the micro to the host. The steps in this process are straightforward. First, the micro makes connection with the host computer. Next, you pretend to edit a new file on the host computer. For example, on a time-sharing-option (TSO) system, you would enter "edit newfile.text". This command would instruct the host computer to open a file called "newfile.text".

The system would respond with the word "Input". Normally, you would begin typing data into this file on the host. In this case, however, using the emulation software, you can instruct the program to pull a file from the micro and automatically enter it into the file called "newfile.text" on the host. The host editor is tricked into believing that you typed the information from the keyboard. The emulation program types one line of information from the disk, which is followed by a carriage return; the next line is then brought up. Eventually, the entire file has been uploaded to the host system.

An uploading capability can be helpful if you use a combination of the mainframe and the microcomputer to complete a task. For example, suppose that you are using 1-2-3 on a micro to produce your department's budget forecast for the upcoming year. Once you complete the forecast on your micro, the report must be fed to the host computer for consolidation with other departments' reports. Using the facility just described, you can upload the forecast figures to the host computer for processing without rekeying of data on the mainframe.

Some serious concerns arise, however, when data is uploaded from a microcomputer to a host. These concerns focus mainly on security and data integrity. The risk of uploading data is discussed in more detail in chapter 18.

Direct-connect Terminal Emulation

Another alternative available using terminal emulation is the direct-connect, or hard-wire, approach. Unlike dial-up terminal emulation, which uses modems as the connection vehicle between mainframes and microcomputers, the direct-connect design uses coaxial cable as the connection medium. Direct-connect terminals have several advantages over dial-up terminals: speed, error-checking, and security.

Several large computer manufacturers support direct-connect terminals. One of the more popular such terminals is the IBM 3270 product line. These terminals attach to an IBM host via a coaxial cable, using the bisynchronous (bisynch) communications protocol. Other vendors, such as Hewlett Packard, Digital Equipment Corporation, and Data General, also support direct-connect terminals.

Microcomputers can emulate most, if not all, of these terminals and can make use of the direct hard-wire environment. Like dial-up terminal emulation, the hard-wire approach utilizes a combination of hardware and software at the microcomputer. The IBM 3278 terminal emulation at the micro is accomplished by plugging an emulation circuit board into the micro and activating the emulation software.

The same coaxial cable that connects 3278 terminals can be connected to the emulation circuit board in the micro. Once it is in place, the combination of hardware and software puts the micro into full 3278 emulation mode. The emulation mode becomes a value-added feature for the microcomputer; all stand-alone microcomputer functions are still available. You can switch between 3278 emulation and stand-alone processing via a technique known as *hot keying.*

For example, you can be signed on to a host session as a 3278 terminal and also have a database program running on the micro. The micro does not, however, process both sessions simultaneously. In effect, when you switch from host to local processing, the host session is suspended until you switch back. The switching is simple: when you press two specified keys simultaneously, the micro will switch from host to stand-alone processing.

The combination of microcomputer processing and intelligent host terminal emulation makes the direct-connect emulation appealing. There are, however, some problems to consider when directly attaching a micro to a host. These concerns span such areas as response-time degradation, security, and cost. These and other issues are discussed in more detail in chapter 9.

DATA INTERCHANGE   As a mainframe-to-micro link alternative, the direct-connect micro offers some advanced features for data interchange. In the dial-up approach, such techniques as data capture and snapshot processing are used to handle downloading of information from host to microcomputer. As discussed earlier, these techniques of file processing are usually adequate only for small amounts of data. Furthermore, both data capture and snapshot processing could result in unwanted information being retrieved. These limitations, and others found in dial-up downloading, are not present with direct-connect terminal emulation.

Assume that you are using a 3278 emulation product at the micro and you want to move data from the host computer to the micro. To exchange data between mainframe and micro, the 3278-emulating microcomputer activates a file-transfer facility while the micro connects to a host session. You must tell the file-transfer utility which file to download and what storage location will be used at the micro. Once this information has been supplied, the file will be brought to the micro and stored in AS-CII format. The process is simple and straightforward.

This approach differs from that used by dial-up communications in that only the file is stored at the micro, not the unwanted characters and symbols associated with some dial-up approaches. The same approach can be used to upload or move data from micro to host computer. Usually, file transfer through direct-connect microcomputers is faster than transfer through dial-up terminal emulation. The chief advantage of direct-connect over dial-up data-transfer techniques is that information does not have to be listed on the screen prior to transfer.

VIRTUAL HOST STORAGE

The mainframe-micro link is continually evolving. From the mainframe point of view, the simplest way to attach microcomputers is to have the micro emulate something that is already supported by the mainframe, which in most cases is the terminal. If the perspective is reversed, and the mainframe-micro link is examined from the point of view of the microcomputer, some different possibilities appear.

From the micro perspective, the easiest way to use the mainframe is for the mainframe to appear as an extension, or peripheral, attached to the micro. If the mainframe could appear as just another disk drive for the micro, data interchange could be accomplished easily. On microcomputers, drive labels A and B are usually reserved for two local disk drives. The drive at the mainframe could be drive C. To attach the micro to the mainframe, however, terminal emulation is still required. If terminal emulation is combined with the external host storage concept, a second mainframe-micro link alternative is produced, known as *virtual host storage* (VHS).

As you have seen, terminal emulation requires special hardware and software at the microcomputer. The mainframe does not have to be altered at all to support terminal-emulating microcomputers. In contrast, the VHS concept for integrating mainframes and microcomputers requires both special software on the mainframe and special hardware and software at the micro.

VHS is much more complex than straight terminal emulation. Because of the deep involvement of the mainframe and its resources, such issues as impact analysis, capacity planning, security, and training should be considered carefully prior to installation of a VHS system. Before these key implementation issues are discussed, some products that use the VHS approach to integrate mainframes and microcomputers will be examined. The products discussed are offered by IBM, Forte Data Systems, and Micro Tempus. Each product uses the concept of VHS, although the actual implementation is somewhat different in each case.

IBM'S VIRTUAL HOST STORAGE   IBM endorses the concept of virtual host storage through the VHS implementation on the System/36. The System/36 is an office minicomputer that can support up to 100 devices, including terminals, printers, plotters, and microcomputers. A single System/36 can be equipped with up to 800 megabytes of hard-disk storage. Special software on the System/36 allows portions of this storage to be used as an extended hard disk for microcomputers.

This virtual storage is completely transparent to the micro's MS-DOS operating system; the System/36 hard disk is seen as just another drive. The virtual disk on the System/36 can be as small as 360KB (equivalent to one floppy diskette) or as large as 32MB.

To protect information on these virtual disks, IBM allows you to specify the drives as *read-only, read/write,* or *no view.* This type of security prevents information on the disk from being inadvertently destroyed or being viewed by unauthorized users.

Once a person at a microcomputer attaches to the virtual drive on the System/36, data transfer is a simple process. The virtual drives are viewed as drive C, D, and so forth. To move data back and forth between the two systems, the DOS COPY command is used. For example, to move FILE_A from drive A on the micro to drive C on the System/36, you would type "COPY A:FILE_A C:FILE_A". Immediately, the information is copied from the physical drive A to virtual drive C on the System/36.

Information from the System/36 virtual drive can also be accessed from within a microcomputer application program. For instance, if you are using a database management program on the microcomputer, the actual database files can reside on the System/36. The virtual drive can move the data straight into the

microcomputer database program. The important thing to remember is that the virtual drive is completely transparent to the
microcomputer operating system and associated application
programs.

FORTE DATA SYSTEMS' VIRTUAL HOST STORAGE

Forte Data Systems offers a high-performance 3278/79 terminal
emulation package for microcomputers. The Forte board allows
microcomputer users not only to have the power and flexibility
of local processing but also to function as a high-speed, full-featured 3278/79 terminal. When equipped with a emulation card,
the microcomputer replaces the 3278/79 terminal.

As mentioned in chapter 9, 3278/79 emulation boards attach
to the mainframe directly via coaxial cables. Forte Data Systems' PJ 3278/79 board is capable not only of emulating a 3278/
79 terminal but also of providing file transfer with IBM mainframes running under VM/CMS, TSO, and CICS. The capabilities of the PJ 3278 board have also been expanded to include a
virtual-host-storage feature, which Forte Data Systems refers to
as Extended Communications Network (EComNet).

EComNet uses a combination of mainframe software and the
PJ 3278/79 boards to achieve the VHS capability. Much as the
virtual storage concept used on the System/36 does, EComNet
extends the vast storage of the mainframe to the microcomputer
level.

The PJ 3278/79 board is attached either locally or remotely to
3274/76 control units, which are connected to the mainframe.
EComNet software operates on a variety of IBM mainframes and
fits easily into the existing IBM mainframe environments. To
attach a microcomputer equipped with the PJ 3278/79 emulation card into the 3270 network, simply disconnect the coaxial
cable attached to a 3278/79 terminal and connect the cable to
the PJ 3278/79 card.

EComNet offers each microcomputer up to 32MB of virtual
storage. Unlike the IBM System/36 approach, which allows the
micro user to specify the size and quantity of virtual storage
areas used, EComNet allows the central data processing department running the mainframe to specify the sizes and quantity
of virtual storage disks. Putting the control at the mainframe

allows greater flexibility in management of disk storage. This concept is sometimes referred to as *capacity management,* a key element in mainframe-micro integration.

The virtual disks at the mainframe are completely transparent to MS-DOS, as well as to programs running on the micro. Information is retrieved or sent to the virtual drive exactly as if it were located at the micro. Several operations are available using the virtual disk, including the capability to mount, dismount, lock, unlock, pass, or scratch a virtual disk.

Besides the virtual storage, which could be used for day-to-day processing or archiving of micro data on the mainframe, EComNet also supports centralized printing on the mainframe. Using the centralize-print facility, you can have access to high-speed printers located at the mainframe; if you need to print a document that would take too long on the local micro printer, that document can be shipped to the mainframe for printing. This facility is not a replacement for local printing, but it offers more flexibility for printing documents created at the micro.

MICRO TEMPUS'S VIRTUAL HOST STORAGE   Micro Tempus is a pioneer in the virtual host storage concept. The company's product, known as Tempus-Link (see figure 11–1), provides virtual storage to microcomputer users. Like the IBM and Forte Data Systems approaches, Tempus-Link allows virtual disks that are several megabytes in size to be created. Once again, this link is completely transparent to the microcomputer.

In one area, however, Tempus-Link does differ greatly from the two approaches discussed earlier. Both IBM and Forte are limited to use with vendor-specific hardware. In the case of IBM, you must be using a System/36 as a host, and only IBM micro-computers can access the virtual storage facility. Forte is also specific in that EComNet requires the PJ 3278/79 emulation card.

Tempus-Link, on the other hand, is not designed around specialized hardware at the microcomputer. The microcomputer can use Tempus-Link through a variety of 3278/79 emulation cards, such as IRMA, FORTE, PCOX, and others. Alternatively, the microcomputer can access Tempus-Link via a dial-up ter-

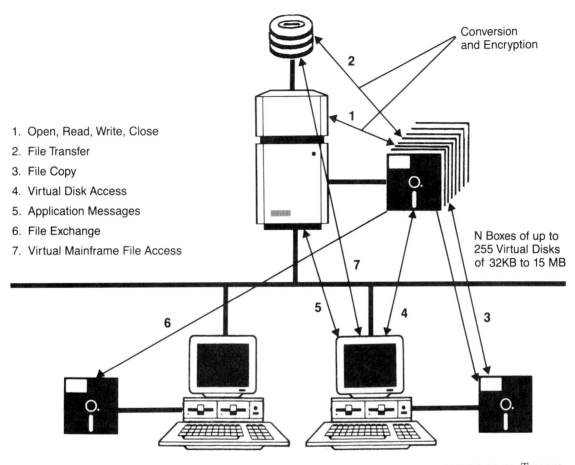

Conversion
and Encryption

1. Open, Read, Write, Close
2. File Transfer
3. File Copy
4. Virtual Disk Access
5. Application Messages
6. File Exchange
7. Virtual Mainframe File Access

N Boxes of up to
255 Virtual Disks
of 32KB to 15 MB

FIGURE 11–1: *Tempus-Link is designed to use mainframe disk storage as a logical extension of the microcomputer environment. Thus, data-storage areas on the mainframe can be used by microcomputer applications software.*

minal-emulation product, such as 3101 or VT-100. In addition, Tempus-Link on the mainframe will work with protocol converters of various types. In effect, Tempus-Link operates independently of the communications used to reach the mainframe. The primary requirement for Tempus-Link is an IBM mainframe running in either an MVS or a CMS environment. Within MVS, Tempus-Link interfaces through the time-sharing option (TSO).

Microcomputer hardware independence permits Tempus-Link to fit into many environments. In addition to virtual storage, other features, such as security and capacity allocation, are supported. Capacity allocation means that the personnel who operate the mainframe can control the allocation of virtual host storage for microcomputer users.

Summary of Virtual Host Storage

The VHS concept is an extremely versatile method of integrating mainframes and microcomputers. It combines the intelligence of local microcomputer workstations with the power and resources available at the mainframe

How the VHS concept is actually implemented and which product is used should be determined by a company's computing environment and end-user requirements. For instance, many central data processing departments are reluctant to open up mainframe storage resources to microcomputer users. For this reason, some departments may choose to use a departmental IBM System/36 as a host rather than implement the software on the main host system. People whose micros are attached to a System/36 can share storage and peripherals on the System/36. The end result is the same: microcomputer storage can be centralized, security can be applied, and the per-workstation cost of the microcomputer can be reduced through shared resource allocation.

In contrast, a company may decide that the best approach is to support virtual storage at the central mainframe. Furthermore, this same company may have previously had a large installed base of IBM 3278 terminals. In addition, it may be decided that if all data were stored in a central location, security and data administration would be better managed. For this environment, the use of the Forte EComNet in conjunction with the PJ 3278/79 boards in microcomputers would be more appropriate.

Over the next few years more mainframe-micro links will appear. Many of these will support the VHS concept. In any mainframe-micro link that involves the use of mainframe resources, however, the impact of the link on the overall mainframe throughput should be analyzed. Furthermore, careful capacity planning at the mainframe must be done if microcomputers are allowed to start using resources that were previously used only by the mainframe. When VHS is made available to microcomputer users, a company may have to double or triple the current number of mainframe disk storage units. This increase in storage capacity must be anticipated.

Equally important, a company should look at security mechanisms on any product under consideration; these mechanisms may vary from excellent to nonexistent. In addition, people must be trained so that they can use the mainframe-micro link in the most efficient way. These and other issues should be addressed prior to the installation of any mainframe-micro link.

DATA EXTRACTION/REPORT WRITER

One method used to close the gap between mainframe data and microcomputer application software is the *data extractor.* For the most part, a data extractor is used to remove or extract information from mainframe databases and/or files.

Data extractors can be product-specific or generalized. A product-specific extractor will extract information from only one environment on the mainframe. For example, a data extractor may be supplied with a database management system on the mainframe. This product-specific extractor can extract information only from the one database system. In contrast, a generalized data extractor can retrieve data from various databases and files. Besides extraction, both approaches will usually provide a reporting interface that puts the extracted data into a cohesive and meaningful format.

The use of extractors/report writers on mainframes is not a new phenomenon. These programs first appeared on the mainframe as a method for supplying data in usable form for terminal users. For years, the only way that information could be removed from a mainframe was through a programmer. A person would submit a request to the data processing department, asking for a particular report. A programmer would then develop a program to generate the needed report.

This procedure kept programmers busy and gave the DP department considerable power in a company; unfortunately, large DP shops could not respond to the demands quickly enough. The resulting frustration led to the advent of simple, menu-driven programs that let people request their own reports and required no special programming skills. The use of these tools on number of mainframe disk storage units. This increase in storage capacity must be anticipated.

Extracting data at the micro is much more complex than it may appear. For instance, the microcomputer complicates the issues of data extraction by raising such issues as security, data-transfer techniques, data translation into microcomputer formats, etc.

Security is a major concern. Once the information is stored on a floppy disk, it can easily be removed from the company. Furthermore, data integrity is a serious concern if microcomputers are allowed to extract, store, and manipulate data from the mainframe. Financial data can be extracted from a mainframe and then manipulated at the micro using an electronic spreadsheet. After that manipulation, there are two sets of numbers, one on the mainframe and one at the micro — which set of numbers is correct? These issues are not unique to data extraction, but they are concerns that must be addressed with regard to mainframe-micro link philosophies.

Despite security and data-integrity questions, the demand for mainframe data at the micro level led to the mainframe-micro data extractor link. In effect, the same software technology used on earlier extractor/report writers on mainframes was modifed to meet the needs of the new microcomputer population. These links provide the capabilities of data extraction, summarization, security, reporting, data translation, file transfer, and many other features necessary to complete the link between mainframe data and the microcomputer.

One of the leading companies in the use of data-extractor technology is Informatics General Corporation. Using a combination of mainframe software and micro software in a product called Micro/Answer, Informatics provides the capability to extract mainframe data, translate it into the proper microcomputer application format, and subsequently transfer the results to microcomputer storage media.

The Micro/Answer system is composed of three steps. First, you specify the desired information; second, Micro/Answer extracts the information from the mainframe database; and third, Micro/Answer creates a report in the desired format. In a single request, you can retrieve data from as many as ten databases.

Micro/Answer can retrieve data from virtually any file or data-management system supported on IBM mainframes. You are not limited to a product-specific or application-specific database.

Once the database is selected, Micro/Answer will give you a list of the available fields within the database. Fields can be chosen by placing the cursor next to the desired field and pressing the Enter key or by typing the field name in the field-selection screen. A list of selected fields is maintained on the screen during this selection process. After the fields are selected, you can specify additional selection criteria to further refine the desired output. Here, Micro/Answer offers information to help you define the selection criteria. Once the criteria are set, you specify how that information should be grouped or organized.

Next, the request is sent to the mainframe computer. The Micro/Answer system opens the micro-mainframe session. At the mainframe, Micro/Answer searches the database, finds the desired information and creates the report (summarization). The report is then downloaded from the mainframe to the micro. To use the extracted information with a specific microcomputer software package, the report must be adapted to the desired format.

Security and Data Integrity

Visi/Answer secures the integrity of data by prohibiting uncontrolled updates of mainframe databases. In addition, Visi/Answer user profiles allow DP supervisors to limit the information each person can access. These profiles limit the scope of user access at four different levels: database, segment, field, and value. With Visi/Answer, you see only the data authorized by the DP management. The user profile also contains any passwords and identifiers needed to access the system. Password protection of Visi/Answer operates both at the personal computer and at the mainframe.

Visi/Answer provides many ways for data processing to control processing and reduce costs. Included in user profiles are a number of processing options, such as classifications that allow the processing of multiple tasks in batches. Batching tasks saves database I/O and reduces CPU use.

Components of the System

The Micro/Answer system contains three parts: Micro/Answer on the microcomputer, the Answer/DB extractor on the mainframe, and a communication line between the micro and the mainframe.

Micro/Answer keeps you from having to translate micro commands to mainframe ones; it also makes it unnecessary for you to have in-depth knowledge of communications and mainframe databases. All you need to know is what information is needed and how to use Micro/Answer to get it.

The Answer/DB extractor does all the mainframe work. It handles security, database access, and scheduling. It services requests, processing them immediately or batching them to save computer cycles and allowing the DP department to control access to the data and to other valuable computer resources.

Once the data are extracted, they are stored until you request them through Micro/Answer. When you request the data, the extractor sends them to your microcomputer. You then use Micro/Answer to convert the transmitted data to a Microcomputer format.

All of the transfers between the two programs are done using 3270-type synchronous or dial-up communications. Different Micro/Answer disks are required for each type of communications, but the same Answer/DB extractor handles both.

The data extractor/report writer allows you to pull data from the mainframe under certain qualifying conditions. You are allowed to summarize the data, to translate the data into the proper format, and to communicate that as a summarized file down to the microcomputer. At that point the data are ready to use.

There are various databases on the mainframe. You want to be able to extract data that meet certain conditions and to be able to summarize the data into a format that is manageable by the PC. You don't want to pull down data that is larger than the available PC storage will support. Some packages let you set up the criteria for selection and summarization interactively, talking to a program on the mainframe. Micro/Answer's approach is to let you develop all of your summarization criteria off-line at the micro. You request a database and fields under specific conditions and then ask for the report to be summarized. Next, you send that request, or task, up to the mainframe, where it is processed.

Thus, the task of extraction can be done off-line at the PC or on-line, depending on the software that performs the extraction. Usually, data-extraction software will go one step further. As it brings the data to the micro, it will ask into which micro format the data should be converted.

Summary of Data Extraction

Informatics, the company that produces Micro/Answer, has targeted Micro/Answer as a data-extraction tool. Because of a strategic or philosophical decision by the company as to how micros and mainframes should be integrated, Micro/Answer offers no uploading capabilities.

The Micro/Answer approach is interesting because of the firm statement it makes about how mainframe-micro interfaces should be limited. If a company agrees with this philosophy, believing that uploading should not even be a possibility, Micro/Answer is an appealing product.

12. Integrated Software

DATA translation is an important requirement of the mainframe-micro link. Mainframe data is typically not usable by microcomputer software packages without some modification. A translation routine must be put into place to provide the needed bridge or conversion between mainframe and micro data formats.

Microcomputers have sparked a whole new generation of powerful and easy-to-use software. Many data requirements of large companies cannot be satisfied, however, by the storage or processing capability of the microcomputer. Thus, some data must be handled by a mainframe computer, and subsets of those data may be processed at the micro. This situation often forces people to learn two software packages, one for processing at the micro and the other for mainframe processing. That, in turn, creates the requirement for data translation between the mainframe and micro.

One way to eliminate these problems is to use the same software on microcomputers and mainframes. Programs that run across a variety of hardware levels — mainframe to micro — are categorized as *integrated software*. Actually, the mainframe and micro versions differ internally. But the user interface, com-

mands, and functionality are identical, and data can move between environments without modification.

INTEGRATED SOFTWARE

With integrated software, a specific applications package can be
run on whatever class of hardware is dictated by your requirements and available computing environment. In some instances, it might be better to have a minicomputer handle the
processing; in others, a micro would be better. Integrated software gives you more flexibility in your choice of processing
equipment.

Integrated software also gives you tighter control over data
compatibility from mainframe to micro. If you're running the
same software package at the mainframe and at the micro, it's
easy to move data back and forth between the two systems.

STAND-ALONE MICROCOMPUTER INTEGRATION

The term *integrated software* can be confusing, because it also
has a second commonly accepted meaning. This meaning relates
strictly to the microcomputer. On a stand-alone micro, integrated software provides an environment in which files created
using various applications — word processing, graphics, spreadsheets, and database managers — can be merged or shared (see
figure 12–1). The concept of integrated software at the micro is
found in such software programs as Symphony, by Lotus Development Corporation, and Framework, by Ashton-Tate.

Stand-alone micro "integration" focuses on integrating one
application with another. The micro-mainframe integration
packages focus on integrating different hardware environments,
using software and communications as the bridge. Micro integration, however, is important to the mainframe-micro link.
When data are transferred from the mainframe to the micro,
they may be needed in several different applications; using these
data in different software packages is easier when data is brought

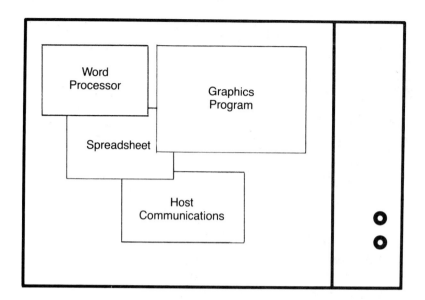

FIGURE 12–1: *Micro integrated software allows users to manipulate several software applications simultaneously. Data from one application can be transferred to another application without translation.*

into an integrated micro environment. Over the past few years, both types of integrated software have become popular.

Many business professionals use electronic spreadsheets, database management systems, graphics programs, and word processors. They typically buy an electronic spreadsheet from one software vendor and then purchase their next program from a different source. When they want to interchange data between the two programs, they are often prevented from doing so due to differences in data formats.

One possible solution to this dilemma is to use programs from one vendor only. Conceptually, this could facilitate the use of a standard interchange format and common commands, thus supporting true integration. This line of thought has led to the advent of micro integrated software.

One of the leading software programs sold today is designed around the integrated software environment. Lotus 1-2-3, by Lotus Development Corporation, offers an electronic spreadsheet, graphics, and database management. The use of such a product enables users to share data between applications easily. Lotus 1-2-3 has been responsible for the sales of many microcomputers. Since the introduction of Lotus 1-2-3, Lotus Development Corporation has expanded its philosophy of integrated software by offering more advanced products: Symphony for the IBM micro world and Jazz for Apple's Macintosh computer.

The major enhancements in Symphony and Jazz are the inclusion of more software applications. Besides the applications used in 1-2-3, Symphony and Jazz support telecommunications and word processing. Also, the existing 1-2-3 features have been expanded. For instance, the Symphony spreadsheet now has more than 8,000 rows, compared to the 2,048 found in 1-2-3.

Since the introduction and success of Lotus' 1-2-3 and Symphony, several other software vendors have adopted this integrated philosophy. Framework, by Ashton-Tate, supports the integrated approach by offering electronic spreadsheet, database management, graphics, word-processing, and telecommunications capabilities. The integrated packages on the market all share some of the same objectives:

- To provide common commands among different applications.
- To permit the sharing of data among different applications.
- To provide applications support through one vendor.

These objectives have contributed to the success of integrated software.

There are, however, some drawbacks to the microcomputer integrated software approach. First, the applications used in the product are not all equally functional. For instance, most database management programs found within an integrated package will not measure up to a dedicated database program. The same is true of the graphics, word-processing, and telecommunication programs found in integrated packages. The one exception to this statement has been the electronic spreadsheet. The capabilities found in current integrated electronic spreadsheets match or surpass those of stand-alone spreadsheet programs.

Before purchasing an integrated package, you should consider the price you pay in lost functionality. For some people, any loss is intolerable. In addition, some people don't like the idea of being locked into one vendor. These concerns have led to the concept of the microcomputer *integrated environment.*

An integrated environment allows the user to integrate applications from a single or multiple vendors. This means that a user can purchase the best programs available in a variety of areas and integrate them on the screen as one common environment. Two products that support this concept are DESQ, from Quarterdeck Software, and Topview, from IBM. These products allow the concurrent use of several programs at once.

INTEGRATED CAPACITY

As the need and desire for integration increases, so will the need for more memory in stand-alone microcomputers. Many people are surprised to learn that after they have loaded all their integrated applications into a microcomputer's memory, there is little memory left for actual processing. So, along with integrated software and integrated environments has come the next generation of microcomputers with much more memory.

MAINFRAME-MICRO INTEGRATED SOFTWARE

To return to the initial definition of integrated software, it would certainly be nice if it were possible to use the same database management software on a mainframe that is used on the microcomputer. People could use a single set of common commands whether they were working in the mainframe or the micro environment. The migration of data and data formats between micro and mainframe would be greatly simplified.

Case 1

Suppose that Joe Smith in accounting loves the multiple capabilities of 1-2-3. Joe's next project involves more than 5,000 records, but that is too much data to be processed on his microcomputer. He would prefer to run this in 1-2-3, but he can't because of the size limitation. Joe's problem could be solved if 1-2-3 were also available in a version that could be run on his IBM 370 mainframe.

Case 2

Suppose that, believing that the application could never outgrow the micro, you develop an application on a micro using micro software, such as dBASE III. Then your department is merged with another department or your business expands. Suddenly the database, which has run satisfactorily on the microcomputer, has grown to a size where the micro can no longer handle it. Now you need to upgrade that system to the minicomputer, or perhaps to the mainframe. Without integrated software, you must rewrite the entire application for the new hardware; if you were using integrated software, you could move your whole system and process it on the new machine without modification.

If the same application programs were used on both mainframes and micros, there would be no need for translation routines to convert mainframe data into microcomputer formats. In addition, if common communications interfaces were built in, the flow of this information would become a much simpler task. These potential benefits have led to the popular mainframe-micro link philosophy known as integrated software.

Again, keep in mind the differences between integrated software at the micro and mainframe-micro integrated software. The micro philosophy concentrates on the integration or sharing of information at the micro level only. In contrast, the mainframe-micro integrated software approach focuses on the integration of data and applications across hardware environments.

One of the first companies to implement the mainframe-micro integrated software approach is Information Builders, which produces FOCUS and its micro counterpart, PC/FOCUS. The FOCUS product consists of a database manager, a financial modeling program, a report writer, a graphics package, and a file-transfer interface. The primary use of the system is to create databases, maintain them, and report on them, using a database management system. Within the FOCUS environment, a variety of sophisticated reports can be developed from the database. PC/FOCUS at the micro uses these same capabilities.

PC/FOCUS at the micro can be connected with FOCUS at the mainframe (see figure 12–2). This allows micros access to the mainframe database. FOCUS continues to control all accesses and regulate the traffic. You can also use PC/FOCUS to manage a local database.

The hardware connection between the mainframe and the mi-

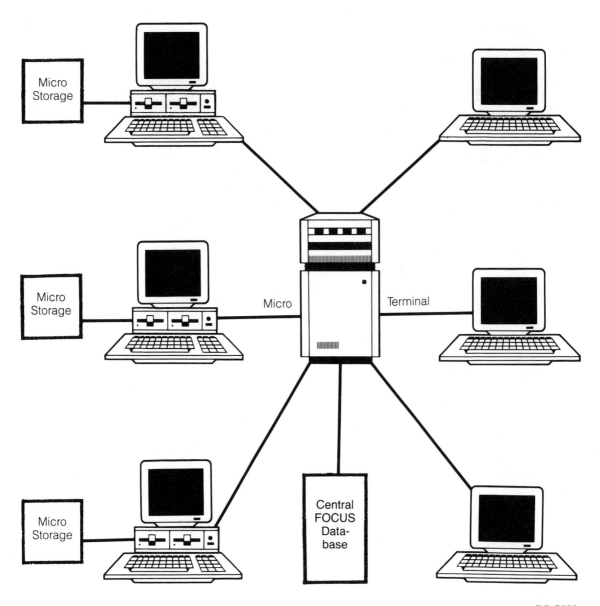

Micro Storage

Micro

Terminal

Central FOCUS Data-base

FIGURE 12–2: *FOCUS supports a distributed processing environment by providing versions of the same software for mainframes and micros. Each of these versions can be interconnected.*

cro can be made by installing a 3270 emulation circuit board in the microcomputer or through authorized dial-up access.

The IBM Approach

The concept of integrated software is a primary objective within IBM's future software directions. Its stated goal is to be able to move documents and data across any environment without having to change the data. To accomplish this task, a common vehicle must be used across hardware environments. For IBM, this vehicle is comprised of several elements, including SNA for communications protocol, DCA for document architecture control, and commonality among software applications regardless of specific hardware.

One of IBM's initial moves toward commonality is in the text-processing field. The text-processing software originally found on IBM's dedicated word processor, the Displaywriter, has been revamped and made available across a variety of IBM hardware groups. The complete line of IBM microcomputers and the System 3X, 43XX, and 30XX families of products support a version of the new text-processing product, known as DisplayWrite. No matter what pieces of IBM hardware you use, your text-processing software can remain the same. This provides the ability for a company to standardize, not only at the hardware level but also at the software level.

Integrated Financial Planning System (IFPS)

Execucom, a leader in the field of decision-support software, has also joined the integrated software market. The company's biggest success is its Interactive Financial Planning System (IFPS), which has enjoyed considerable acceptance in the mainframe world. IFPS provides the capability of using models for financial analysis, a feature that is similar to spreadsheets found on micros. Because IFPS was initially designed to be a mainframe-based software tool, it has an inherent capability to manipulate large amounts of data. The models produced in IFPS can be combined, cross-linked, consolidated, and so forth. The consolidation feature could be used by a corporate office to consolidate financial information from divisions automatically at predetermined times.

In many cases, the power of a product such as IFPS is not needed, and a simple micro financial spreadsheet is sufficient. Many companies use micro-based spreadsheets to complement IFPS. One of the obvious disadvantages of using two products in this manner is that you're required to learn one set of commands for the micro spreadsheet program and a completely different set for the software on the mainframe. In addition, the interaction or transmission of data from two different programs is often difficult. To address these problems, Execucom developed IFPS/Personal.

IFPS/Personal is a microcomputer version of the IFPS package that runs on mainframes. In essence, with IFPS and IFPS/Personal, you have one set of commands and one common interface. IFPS/Personal is of particular interest to companies that already have IFPS on a mainframe and now are experiencing an influx of microcomputers. The combination of the two software products creates a powerful mainframe-micro decision-support link.

SUMMARY

Mainframe-micro integrated software offers some tremendous benefits over other approaches. With integrated software it doesn't matter at which level of hardware you're working — the data are totally compatible, the keystrokes are the same, and the menus are the same. Migration from system to system is easy. Integrated software is being developed for all of the major software areas, including database management, graphics, spreadsheets, and word processing.

The integrated software movement could have an effect on the acceptance of particular microcomputer software programs in large companies. Integrated software definitely helps to enforce standardization of software programs throughout a company, at all hardware levels. In addition, integrated software can reduce the training and support demands.

Integrated packages will probably be accepted first at the departmental level, with micros and minis using the same software. Already IBM has developed the departmental integrated software approach with its System/36 departmental mini system, which runs the same software as the IBM microcomputers. Other vendors, such as Wang and AT&T, are also implementing this technique.

An example of using this approach would be a company that has a financial modeling program that runs on micros and on minis, with the mini version offering a few more advanced features, such as consolidation. If each departmental spreadsheet were done independently, these spreadsheets could be sent to the minicomputer, where the mini version could consolidate them all into one report.

13. Modems and Protocol Converters

TWO of the most common telecommunications transport vehicles are the modem and the protocol converter. Each of these transport alternatives plays a major role in mainframe-to-micro connection strategies.

The modem is an integral part of the mainframe-to-micro illustrations throughout this book and is just as prevalent in actual installations. A modem derives its name from its function: it MOdulates and DEModulates communications data streams. A modem takes digital transmissions and converts them to analog transmissions, then performs the process in reverse. This process allows computers to communicate using standard telephone lines. Telephone lines are capable of transmitting both voice and data. Information is moved across these phone lines through a technique known as analog transmission. Computers move and process information using digital signals.

When information is stored on one computer and must be transmitted to another computer across telephone lines, something must be used to convert the digital signals of the computer into analog signals that allow the information to be transmitted across the telephone line. In addition, once the transmission is received on the other end, something must convert those same analog signals back into a digital form in order for the receiving

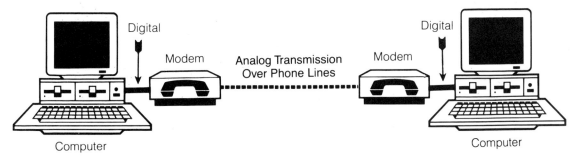

Computer   Computer

computer to interpret it properly. This is the function performed by the modem (see figure 13–1).

FIGURE 13–1: *Modems are used for analog/digital conversion to permit communications between computers using standard telephone lines. The conversion is necessary because computers normally generate digital signals, whereas telephone lines are adapted to handle analog signals.*

MODEM TRANSMISSION RATES

Modems operate at a variety of transmission rates. In telecommunications terms, these rates are referred to as baud rates. (*Baud* is the common measurement unit for modems and is roughly equivalent to bits per second.) The typical transmission rates for modems are 300, 1200, 2400, 4800, and 9600 baud.

Choice of transmission rates should be based on several criteria: transmission protocol, cost considerations, and compatibility with receiving modem. The transmission protocol in the mainframe-micro link could be X.25, SNA/SDLC, asynchronous, synchronous, bisynchronous, or many others. Each of these protocols supports a full range of communication speeds, although there are some practical limits.

As has been mentioned, standard asynchronous communications do not provide for error checking and recovery. Because of this, relatively low transmission speeds should be used to maintain data integrity. Normally, speeds ranging from 300 to 1200 baud are used in conjunction with asynchronous communications. Higher-speed modems can be used with modified asynchronous communication protocols, such as XMODEM or BLAST. Because these protocols add error-checking and recovery techniques, higher-speed transmission will not threaten overall data integrity.

Cost and speed are directly related. Faster speed means higher modem cost. Modems that transmit at 1200 baud cost between $200 and $700, depending on the features and the manufacturer. At the other end of the spectrum, a 9600-baud modem costs between $2,000 and $4,000.

Of course, the basic modem price is only one part of the cost analysis. Faster modems may increase workstation productivity substantially. In addition, higher-speed modems are often used to support multiple terminals or microcomputers through a single telephone line. This technique, called *multidrop*, is frequently used with local area networks and communications controllers. Multidropping through a single high-speed modem may have a relative cost per workstation that is less than that for supplying each workstation with a dedicated modem.

Matching modems on both sides of the transmission link is critical. The speed of the modem connected at the receiving computer must exactly match the transmission speed of the transmitting modem. If a mainframe communications front-end is equipped with 1200 baud modems, workstations cannot use 2400 baud modems to contact the mainframe.

Another compatibility consideration is protocol implementation. Many modem manufacturers enhance the standard protocol for better data integrity or security. This is especially common with asynchronous modems, which may have built-in data-integrity enhancements. Normally, the receiving and transmitting modem must be made by the same manufacturer in order for the enhancements to function properly.

PROTOCOL CONVERTERS

Analysts, systems integrators, and MIS managers usually strive for standardization whenever possible in communications systems. Frequently, though, standardization is impossible, and many types of computers and communications technologies must be integrated into a single system. Technological diversity has many causes. In some instances, the evolution of personnel has resulted in a mixture of installed hardware and software systems. In other cases, market trends, technological innovation, and changing end-user requirements have left some companies with tremendous integration challenges. Because there are often few standards that are common to different manufacturers, integration can be difficult.

Only recently have computer and communications manufacturers made measurable progress in developing standards that facilitate integration. Industry standards, however, normally take years to mature and replace existing systems. In the meantime, MIS professionals are still faced with the challenge of integrating different computer and communications technologies.

The most common approach used in integration is at the communications level. Fortunately, the communications field has produced some standards from which integration can build. Most computer systems support the EIA RS-232-C communications connection. Through this communications vehicle, protocols such as asynchronous, X.25, and SNA can communicate with one another between different computer systems. A hardware connection, such as RS-232-C, is only a part of the communications puzzle. The other involves software interfaces (software protocols). The key to effective communications between computers is the matching of both ends.

In some cases, an originating computer may support only the asynchronous communication protocol, whereas the receiving computer is expecting the SNA protocol. This conflict is much like the difficulty people have in communicating when the speaker uses English and the listener understands only French. Like humans, computers cannot communicate successfully unless both ends speak the same language, that is, use the same protocol.

For humans, the bridge between languages is a translator, someone who understands both languages and can converse back and forth in each person's native language. The same approach is used in computer and communications technologies. In the technical world this translation is performed by a combination of hardware and firmware known as a protocol converter. A protocol converter translates one communications protocol into another. Without such a device, communications between unlike equipment and protocols would be impossible. A protocol converter can integrate computers, irrespective of size or manufacturer.

Companies who wish to connect microcomputers to a host computer have three fundamental choices. Two possible choices are to use dedicated cables or dial-up lines and to match the communication protocol supported by the vendor. The 3270/IBM host connection is an example of this kind of connection; both dedicated cable and dial-up lines are supported by the 3270.

If a company already has an installed base of workstations and subsequently purchases a host computer from another manufacturer, it should consider a third alternative — using protocol converters. The most common protocol conversion is from asynchronous to synchronous communications. A company with a large installed base of asynchronous terminals will normally use protocol converters to permit the terminals to communicate with the synchronous mainframe environment. When microcomputers are brought in as additional workstations, they will often be connected to the same async terminal system. (See figure 13–2 for some possible installations of protocol converters.)

Protocol converters are available with a wide variety of capabilities. Their selection is usually based on the number of ports required, the protocols that must be integrated, and the desired transmission speed. As with most other computer-related systems, managers should standardize on one vendor and model of protocol converter. Each model has its own unique user interface, and it is preferable to have only one such interface for a computing environment.

Protocol converters do have some drawbacks. Because they use telephone lines, the speed of the system is usually slower than it would be with dedicated wiring. Also because telephone lines are used, the company will incur line-use charges from the telephone company — often a significant cost.

Finally, the protocol converter is often purchased to solve the problem of matching equipment from different vendors. The protocol converter itself is usually from yet another vendor, however, and this adds to the complexity of the system. When something goes wrong, for example, the vendors may accuse one another's equipment of causing the problem, making it difficult to find a cure.

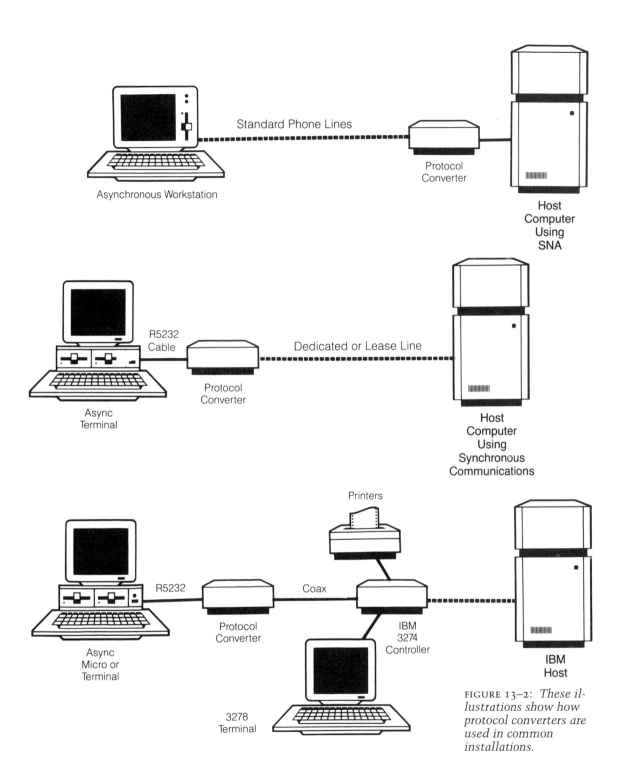

Standard Phone Lines

Protocol
Converter

Asynchronous Workstation

Host
Computer
Using
SNA

R5232
Cable

Dedicated or Lease Line

Protocol
Converter

Async
Terminal

Host
Computer
Using
Synchronous
Communications

Printers

R5232

Coax

Protocol
Converter

IBM
3274
Controller

Async
Micro or
Terminal

3278
Terminal

IBM
Host

FIGURE 13–2: *These illustrations show how protocol converters are used in common installations.*

Case Analysis

Over the years, a company has installed several minicomputers from such companies as Hewlett-Packard, Data General, and DEC. Along with the minicomputers, a forest of associated terminals, microcomputers, and printers has appeared in user work areas. As the company grew in size and complexity, the company's top management, in conjunction with the MIS department, decided to centralize all computer operations around an IBM mainframe. It was decided that all applications being run on minicomputers would be converted and that the machines would be sold. It was also decided that all terminals and printers were to remain and somehow be integrated into the IBM system. This left the company with quite a challenge.

The MIS department spent the next two years carrying out this plan. At the end of the two years, all applications had been converted onto the IBM mainframe. A major problem still existed in how to connect the non-IBM workstations to the new system. The majority of the workstations previously used on the microcomputers were asynchronous devices. Because the IBM system supported only the bisynchronous and the SNA/SDLC protocols, the challenge was how to marry the installed base of asynchronous devices into the IBM world.

This situation is a classic example of a case in which protocol converters could be used. Several of the protocol converters on the market can convert the asynchronous protocol into SNA/SDLC and bisynchronous protocols. The company could install several of these protocol converters (all from the same vendor) in front of the IBM mainframe. The asynchronous devices could dial up the computer or use a leased line and appear to the mainframe as an SNA or bisynchronous terminal.

The same benefits can be realized by using protocol converters as bridges between mini or departmental mini systems and workstations. Most minicomputer manufacturers support only a limited number of terminals and protocols on their systems. A company could enjoy much greater flexibility in workstation selection if a protocol converter that permits the connection of standard asynchronous devices were used. The protocol converter could then convert the asynchronous devices into a protocol expected by the receiving minicomputer system.

SUMMARY

Modems perform digital-to-analog conversion of computer transmissions so that these transmissions can use standard telephone lines. Of primary consideration when selecting a modem is the speed and brand of the modem at the other end of the communications line. Modems can only communicate with other modems that have identical baud rates. The manufacturer of the modem is a consideration if a special feature must be supported; that is, an error-checking modem can work only with a similar modem.

Protocol converters are used to connect between two otherwise incompatible communications devices. The most common reason for using protocol converters is to allow previously installed equipment to be integrated into new systems. In effect, the protocol converter allows a company to purchase computers and terminals based on capabilities rather than compatibilities.

14. Telecommuni-
cations and the
PABX

OFTEN when mainframe-micro integration strategies are developed, the telephone system is ignored. For many people, the telephone system is merely the devices that sit on their desks, into which they talk. Individuals may use their voice phone lines to connect a terminal or microcomputer in order to communicate with another computer, but even these uses are just extensions of the past telecommunication capabilities found in simple voice-only phone systems.

Today's telephone systems offer a multitude of features and capabilities never before found in a telephone system. Often these computer-oriented features go unnoticed by people who would never think to look for computer capabilities in a telephone system. It's important for a company to realize that modern telephone systems can and should serve as an integral part of an office automation or mainframe-micro integration strategy.

THE EVOLUTION OF THE TELEPHONE

For decades, the telephone industry was monopolized by AT&T. The break-up of AT&T and the deregulation of the telephone industry in the early 1980s, however, has permitted more competition. Discount rates on long-distance calls were the first result of the break-up; local phone companies have also reduced their long-distance rates in order to be competitive. However, the cost of local calls has risen sharply.

Today's rapid growth in the number of telephone companies, combined with advances in communications and computer technology, has led to what is called the telecommunications industry. Users are no longer confined to just a simple voice phone system, using manual switch operators and huge air-conditioned rooms.

Several companies have emerged as leading manufacturers in the telecommunications field. Some of these companies are NEC, ROLM, ZTEL, United Technologies, Northern Telecom, AT&T, and GTE. These are manufacturers of telephone systems, also known as *telephone switches.*

Telephone switches are often referred to as private automatic branch exchanges, or PABXs. The sophistication of the PABX allows a company to become its own phone company in many ways. With older phone systems, if an individual moved from one office to another, the phone company typically would have to be notified to relocate the phone number to the new office. Today, the power to move instruments and to change phone numbers is in the hands of the customer. From a special terminal, a person can instantly change the location of a telephone number, without the assistance of the phone company.

Some of the more advanced PABX switches allow a person to unplug his phone, carry it to a new office location, plug it in and notify the switch of the move through a command from the phone. The control that a company has over its own communications network has made the modern PABX a desired resource.

In the 1970s, phone systems were primarily voice-only systems. During the same period, data networks and sophisticated mainframe computers dominated the data world. The end of the 1970s saw a trend from analog to the much more efficient digital PABX systems. In addition to digital transmission, the end of the 1970s brought expanded use of microwave, satellite, and computer network technologies.

The early 1980s have set the stage for some of the most exciting advancements in the telecommunications field. The integration of voice and data in a single communications processor is now spreading across the industry. *Integration* is one of the key words of the 1980s in telecommunications as well as the computer industry.

The last half of this decade is producing the integration of sophisticated digital PABX systems with integrated computer systems. The telecommunications industry is rapidly merging with the computer field. Each of these large industries needs the other to move forward. Two of the largest companies in the world, AT&T and IBM, are locked in a competitive struggle to dominate these converging technologies. Both companies can be expected to do much to bring the technologies together at a faster rate than previously anticipated.

IBM'S MOVE INTO TELECOMMUNICATIONS

For decades IBM has dominated the computer industry. First, IBM mainframes and terminals set the standards by which others have followed; next, IBM's move into the microcomputer field was equally strong. With the telecommunications and computer technologies coming together, however, IBM's dominance has been threatened. Although IBM does manufacture some communications equipment, used to tie together its computers and terminals, much more sophisticated telecommunications equipment, including systems for both voice and data transmission, are required. Faced with two choices — starting from scratch to develop its own telecommunications equipment or acquiring an existing telecommunications company — IBM chose to acquire the telecommunications expertise. The company began this move by buying a small stake in ROLM, one of the leading telecommunications, or telephone-switching, companies. In late 1984, IBM announced that it was acquiring ROLM. For years experts speculated about the merger of computer technology and communications; IBM's move to acquire ROLM made the notion a reality.

The move to buy ROLM corporation directly affected IBM's primary telecommunications competitor, AT&T. However, AT&T was also broadening its capabilities.

AMERICAN TELEPHONE & TELEGRAPH

The break-up of AT&T in 1984 was of extreme significance. First, it split AT&T into smaller business units. As mentioned earlier, the deregulation also allowed competitors to enter the phone business. Internally, AT&T has used high-speed computers for several years; AT&T's Bell Laboratories also created the widely used UNIX operating system. Until deregulation occurred, AT&T had been prohibited from entering the computer field on a commercial basis. Immediately after the break-up, AT&T announced its entry into the computer field; that announcement was followed by the introduction of a computer line, including a microcomputer known as the 6300, which is IBM-compatible and runs the AT&T UNIX operating system. In early 1985, the 7300 microcomputer was introduced to expand AT&T's microcomputer product line. In addition, supermicros such as the 3B2 and a powerful mini system known as the 3B5 were released.

AT&T's success in the telecommunications field does not necessarily guarantee success in the highly competitive computer industry. While building its product line and reputation in the computer field, AT&T will have to confront IBM — no small challenge. Because of AT&T's particular expertise in the UNIX world, its computer products should do well in the science and engineering arenas. Overall, the AT&T line of products simply cannot be ignored. By blending its decades of telecommunications expertise with highly respected computer systems, AT&T could rise to become IBM's biggest competitor in the future.

MERGING PABX TECHNOLOGY WITH THE COMPUTERS

The days of the simple voice telephone system are disappearing rapidly. Sophisticated PABX systems are being installed in large and small companies. These systems not only serve to provide high-quality voice transmission but become integrated components of a company's system architecture. Because today's PABX systems support voice and data, and in some cases simultaneous transmission, their use in conjunction with computer systems is a natural marriage.

Phone systems normally function as the first vehicle in a company to tie together not only individuals but also computers. Although most phone lines are designed primarily to handle voice transmission, low-speed data transmissions also can travel over standard voice lines without much difficulty.

As the use of distributed computing systems rises, so does the need for high-speed, high-quality data transmission. When faced with these requirements, most companies lease specially conditioned lines from the phone company. With the use of modern PABX systems, internal data transmission at high speeds can be accomplished without the assistance of the phone company and without special leased lines. The PABX can be used to connect computer systems and to serve as a first-generation local area network, in many cases.

A major benefit of telecommunications is that the telephone system can be used to connect dissimilar computers. Using a modem and a simple RS-232-C connector, two different computers can communicate via a phone line. The modem is used to convert the analog transmission of the phone network to digital transmission that the computer can understand. Modern PABX technology has negated the need to use modems to communicate with computers that are interconnected through the switch or PABX. Because the PABX, unlike older phone systems, is digital, there is no need for the conversion that the modem would otherwise provide.

In effect, if a company has a modern digital PABX system, terminals, microcomputers, and computers can be directly connected to the phone systems without a modem. This is typically done by equipping the desktop telephone with a standard RS-232-C connector. A simple cable is then run from the serial port on the computer to this RS-232-C connector. Once the connection is made, the computer can be used to dial any computer connected to the PABX. An advanced feature found on most switches is the ability to conduct simultaneous voice and data transmissions from a single phone set.

Besides using the data capabilities of the PABX to communicate from computer to computer, a user can take advantage of a feature known as *modem pooling*, which allows computers connected to the switch to share a central group of modems. The modems in the modem pool are used to communicate to computers that are not physically connected to the PABX.

THE PABX ON A LAN

Future advances in technology will lead to sophisticated multi-purpose local area networks. In the early stages of system integration, however, the PABX will serve as a connection vehicle for voice and data requirements. As the industry moves ahead, the use of such technologies as fiber optics, broadband local area networks, voice-activated systems and others will all be integrated with PABX systems.

Several telecommunications and local area network vendors are developing gateways between broadband local area networks and PABX systems. Through the use of gateways, the PABX becomes a node or participant on the local area network. The merging of broadband technology and PABXs will be a powerful combination. Increasingly, fiber optics will be used to provide high-speed transmissions between PABX systems and local area networks.

The blending of the telecommunications field and computer technology will definitely occur in the near future. Not only must this migration occur in the technical arena, but companies that have separated their communications department from their data processing department must also join the two, or at least make sure they communicate closely.

Both the telecommunications industry and computer manufacturers will offer similar capabilities. Duplication of features in computer system networks and PABX systems must be monitored by consumers. For instance, if a company is installing a broadband local area network through a company or building, there may be no need to implement a sophisticated PABX that offers voice and data. Because the broadband network should handle most data needs, a simple voice-only PABX may suffice, if the PABX is properly linked to the broadband network.

A clear strategic plan involving communications and data processing departments should be developed to ensure sound cost-effective integration.

As for mainframe-micro integration, improved telecommunications methods, hardware, and software will provide a smoother connection vehicle. Remember that in the mainframe-micro integration methodology, telecommunications is the glue that holds all the pieces together.

As PABX switches are equipped with built-in telecommunication protocols, such as X.25 and SNA, the micro will be able to tap into the basic phone set to have access to sophisticated mainframes and minicomputer systems. Small departmental processors will be developed that will not only include data processing capabilities but also serve as a PABX (voice and data) and computer in one functional unit. Most importantly, don't disregard the telephone system when developing an overall mainframe-micro strategy.

PABX IMPLEMENTATIONS

The current PABX technology allows you to interface the computer directly to the telephone, which alleviates the need of having modems at each individual workstation.

Several modems are installed at the PABX, creating a modem pool (see figure 14–1). For 100 people, for example, the modem pool might consist of 30 modems. These people can use the modem pool to dial outside of their environment. To do so, the user first enters a telephone number at the computer. The request goes through the computer and the telephone to the PABX, where an available modem sends the data to the outside world. The system can support data speeds up to 19.2 Kbps, using most of the current PABX devices.

The PABX thus provides an efficient answer for external, wide-area network communications. The next step is to integrate a data communications network with the telephone system. A data communications network can be designed with a PABX attached. Any computer on the network can go through the network to the PABX to communicate with remote computers, but will rely on the communications network for local traffic.

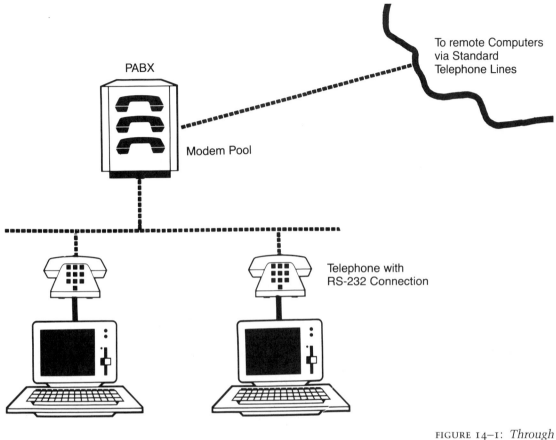

PABX

Modem Pool

To remote Computers
via Standard
Telephone Lines

Telephone with
RS-232 Connection

FIGURE 14–1: *Through the use of a PABX, microcomputers can be interconnected and can share a group of modems known as a modem pool.*

SUMMARY

Using the new PABX technology, the telephone system can be effectively integrated with data systems. Because of this, people in the communications department should do joint planning with those in the computer department. Some of the capabilities of PABXs and data-communications networks now overlap. In any implementation, the two technologies should be considered side by side to avoid buying redundant capabilities.

15. Local Area Networks

THE direct mainframe-micro link offers one solution for delivering data to the micro workstation. It is not necessarily the best solution, however. The mainframe still controls the data, and the micro is often relegated to being little more than a dumb terminal. Capabilities such as data capture, local processing, and remote job entry do improve the workstation's role, but workstations are still highly dependent upon the mainframe — usually more so than is justified. The fundamental problem with a direct mainframe-micro link is that data are removed from the micro workstation environment and stored and managed at a central location.

Data processing systems should be designed according to patterns of use. In most organizations, data- and resource-sharing takes place primarily among members of the same department. In this situation, it's preferable to keep those resources at the department level where they are used. A department-to-mainframe link can be installed to update departmental data as necessary.

Such a strategy has three benefits. It brings data closer to the people who use it, thereby making the data more accessible. It reduces the load on mainframe processing and communications facilities. Finally, it reduces the resource demands on the communications network.

Localizing shared data at the department level can be done through a departmental minicomputer system. Alternatively, organizations can implement a powerful technology designed especially for distributed processing; this technology is called the *local area network.*

THE LOCAL AREA NETWORK

Local area networks, or LANs, tie microcomputers together and allow requests, responses, and messages to be sent among the connected machines and peripherals. LANs are distinguished from other types of communications networks by speed, size, and computing environment. A LAN, traditionally, is a high-speed system that moves data across the network so quickly that you don't notice the difference between network responses and responses from your own local disk drive. This usually requires a cable speed (raw bit rate) of from 1 to 10 megabits per second (Mbs). As the word *local* implies, the size of the LAN is typically limited to a single building or perhaps a campus.

The computing environment is distributed. In a host-to-terminal environment, a computer's central processing unit (CPU) is shared by attached terminals or by micros emulating terminals. In a LAN, a central machine provides communications and disk management for attached micros. Each micro, however, runs its own applications software and processes its own data.

The basic components of a LAN are a cable, network interface cards, and network software. Most LANs contain these three basics, or some functional equivalents. LANs may also have several other networked devices to handle the needs of a particular office. The network interface card (circuit board) is installed in the microcomputer's expansion bus. A cable is routed to all of the microcomputers on the network. Data storage devices (usually hard disks) are shared through one or more microcomputers called *servers.* These server micros run network software that

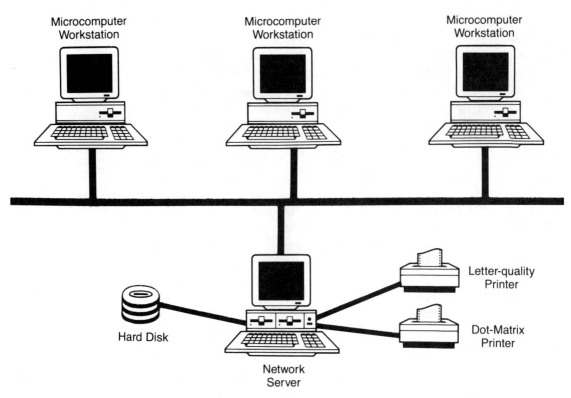

Microcomputer Workstation   Microcomputer Workstation   Microcomputer Workstation

Hard Disk

Letter-quality Printer

Dot-Matrix Printer

Network Server

manages the hard disk and other attached peripherals for the entire network (see figure 15–1).

As an illustration of how a LAN operates, suppose that the hard disk attached to micro workstation A has been designated as a shareable resource for the LAN. The server software running in workstation A maintains storage-area assignments and user profiles. If micro workstation B wants to use the shared hard disk, the request is filtered first through the server to see if the request is authorized. Once the request is approved, it is executed by the server, which then sends the response back to workstation B. The server can receive additional requests from other workstations while it's working on workstation B's request. These requests are placed on temporary hold and answered sequentially after the current request is executed. Requests to printers and other peripherals are handled in much the same way.

FIGURE 15–1: *A local area network provides the means to share peripherals, such as hard disks and printers. It also permits the sharing of information, so that network users can pass documents and other data back and forth. The facilities of the network are controlled by the network server.*

LANs also permit sharing of the same data through a mechanism know as *locking.* A lock lets you stop other people from using a file while you are using it. When only individual records are being updated, as is often done in inventory systems, record locks can be used. These prevent simultaneous access to specified records, but leave the remainder of the file available for updating.

EXPANDING A LAN

LANs have built-in growth capability. Usually, such networks are installed as small systems connecting four or five micros and a hard disk. As the size of the office and the use of computers increase, the LAN can also grow.

One of the first "modular" facilities people get for their LANs is software to support printer sharing (print-server software, in LAN jargon). Printer sharing works on the principle that not everybody uses the printer at the same time, and few people use it for long periods of time. When several people share one printer, their requests will usually come at different times. If one printer request arrives while another request is being processed, the requests can be stacked in a queue, or waiting line, and answered sequentially.

In a typical LAN, any attached micro can share the networked peripherals. The sharing capability becomes especially significant as a way to improve peripheral quality. Large hard disks, back-up systems, high-speed printers, and specialized devices become economical in a shared situation. Quality, performance, and mean time between failure (MTBF) can all be improved, while keeping the per-user cost of peripherals at a realistic level.

THE OFFICE MICRO

The LAN was first created as a way to overcome some of the problems associated with microcomputers. It was found that micros in an office should usually be connected into a system in the same way that people in an office need to work together and communicate. Some of the reasons for interconnecting micros are economic. The micro is a powerful office tool that can do virtually any processing task assigned to it. The micro can also be used to drive a whole stable of peripheral devices, including plotters, modems, hard disks, and both dot matrix and letter-quality printers.

The very richness of opportunities tends to be frustrating. A micro is primarily a single-user workstation, and most businesses cannot justify dedicating many specialized peripherals solely for the use of one individual. Typically, a micro is bought with only an inexpensive dot matrix printer. When other peripherals are acquired, their usage is limited by physical location. For instance, suppose you want to use the letter-quality printer attached to micro number 6. You get up and go to the printer, but because the micro to which the printer is attached is also being used as a workstation, you must wait for a free moment before you can use the printer.

Stand-alone micros in the office have other problems. Some jobs aren't practical at all. For example, distributed processing may work well, but distributed record-keeping usually does not. In a stand-alone environment, everybody may start the morning with inventory disks showing 12 widgets in stock. As soon as any micro enters an order to sell or buy widgets, the data on the other micros becomes invalid and unusable. The same thing occurs with a database of customers. If two or more people are making entries, then nobody's version is valid. Correcting the various versions later is a tedious waste of time.

Another problem with the stand-alone micro is that office automation is hampered by office isolation. Because micro users have so much local capability, they tend to develop their own little world of personalized software packages, utilities, formats, and ways of doing things. It's not uncommon to find a mixture of different word-processing software, spreadsheets, and other applications in one office: one person is using WordStar, another is using MultiMate, and so on. It's even more likely that each person will have a unique set of utilities and will have made his own minor modifications to the applications.

This situation sets up some monstrous incompatibilities — you can't read another person's text file with your word processor, and he can't read your spreadsheet. User support is much more difficult. You can't develop a set of common training procedures or applications tips if everyone is using different software, and when a person has a question or a problem with the software, the supervisor may not be familiar with that particular package.

With a local area network, all applications software can be placed on the central hard disk, from which it can be distributed to the users. This way, everyone is using the same software packages and the supervisor can easily maintain them.

In a normal LAN set-up, the applications software will be available to users on a read-only basis. In other words, the user can load the software from the hard disk and use it to create files, but he cannot modify the software itself. Any user who is attached to the network and has access to that software can use it, even while several other users are also using it. Programs used in this way are commonly referred to as multiuser software.

Although many software packages cannot be installed on a hard disk because of copy protection, it's not difficult to find suitable software. You'll find, too, that if you choose to switch to true multiuser software, there are some other advantages. Multiuser applications software "knows" that it's a shared application, so it usually includes security and data-integrity features not required in a single-user system.

One of the important values of a LAN is that it can bring everyone up to a common level of information. With good multiuser software, information can be merged and maintained easily in a single version that everyone can use.

DISKLESS MICROS

One way to ensure that everyone is using the same applications software and the same information is to set up your office with diskless micros. With a local area network, micros don't necessarily have to have any local storage — local drives — at all. They can be booted directly from the central hard disk. By eliminating the floppy disk drive and drive controller, you can cut the cost of each micro by several hundred dollars.

Diskless micros are also secure. Microcomputers are a ready tool for stealing company data. Just pop in a disk and copy whatever data files you want. Once that data is on a floppy disk, there is literally no way to prevent its going out the door. A diskless micro provides no way to make copies, so the station is secure, at least against large-scale theft.

For many companies, though, the most important reason for using diskless micros is that they stop software piracy. The software industry is close to hysteria on this topic, and they aren't passively wringing their hands, either; they are pursuing several multimillion dollar lawsuits against companies whose employees allegedly distributed bootlegged software. Once a company buys software and registers it, the company becomes responsible for protecting that software against illegal copying. In reality, there is no way to prevent an employee from making copies — unless you remove the copy machine, in this case the disk drive.

The ideal use of diskless micros is in classroom situations and as intelligent data entry terminals. In other places, diskless micros have some obvious drawbacks. For one thing, you can't keep a local back-up, something that may be desirable for non-shared data. Another drawback is that without disk drives all user requests must go on the network. Some files, such as personal notes and scratch pads, are just better kept local. In addition, keeping some data local takes some of the burden off the network and helps maintain better network performance.

LAN COMMUNICATIONS

The uses of LANs discussed above might be classed as organizational. The LAN lets you coordinate micro activity, improve data integrity, and share the cost of high-quality peripherals. The other major area of LAN application is communications.

With a LAN, micros become personal data communications transceivers. They can support two-way communications, one-way information dissemination, and large-scale document delivery, all at electronic speed without the necessity of a delivery person or even hard copy.

Perhaps the most basic of the communications services a LAN offers is that provided by the read-only area of a disk. Most LANs let you designate a particular area as available to all users for information dissemination. People on the network cannot write to the file; they can only read the information. Read-only files have many uses. For example, companies could use this type of file as an electronic newsletter, as a medium to list various general personnel information, or as a client directory.

Usually, when people think of LAN communications, they think of electronic mail. Electronic mail can be defined as a message creation and delivery system supported entirely by electrical signals. In other words, you can use electronic mail packages to write, address, and deliver your messages. The messages can be anything from short memos to letters to long documents. With LAN electronic mail, a message is addressed to someone on the network and stored in a special place on the shared hard disk. The addressee is informed that a message is waiting. The message can then be read at any convenient time.

LAN electronic mail packages often have several other nice features. You can store messages, forward them, or add your own comments to them and forward both. You can also set up a routing system for messages, so that they go to multiple parties.

One of the biggest problems in office communications is getting someone else on the other end of the phone line. You need a fast response, but when will the other person be available to talk to you? Electronic mail permits you to get an idea or request immediately to another person. The response will be either immediate or as soon as the person chooses to respond. Although you may still have to wait for a response, electronic mail need be sent only once — you don't have to keep calling until the person is available.

In this age of telecommuting, a useful application of electronic mail is between a remote micro and the network. Somebody traveling for a company or working at home can receive and send messages from and to anyone on the LAN via the telephone. A new application, still being refined, is internetwork mail. Using internetwork devices, some of which are as simple as a telephone modem, a message can originate on one LAN and be sent to a person on another network. That other network could be in the next department or across the country.

The value of any communications system increases proportionately with the number of people who can use that system. As electronic mail is more and more widely implemented, it will become a significant factor in global communications.

BACK-UP STRATEGY

Reliable back-ups are crucial to protecting data, and this is one of the benefits of a local area network. Back-up is physically possible on stand-alone micros. The tendency, however, is to forget the back-up. For one thing, floppy disk back-up is a considerable amount of work; few people enjoy reviewing all of their work for the day and then swapping floppy disks until it's all backed up. A number of companies have conducted surveys on how well back-up procedures are followed. They have found that back-up tends to be spotty at best. When the workday ends, people want to go home. They don't want to spend time doing some boring administrative chore that they don't perceive as their "real" job anyway.

With a LAN, you can set up a central back-up facility where all the day's work is backed up. This usually means you can justify the cost of a convenient and reliable back-up system, such as a tape drive. The back-up process can be as simple as hitting a button on the back-up unit. Not only is it easy, but one person is tasked with backing up the data. It's not an afterthought; it's one of a series of procedures specifically assigned to the person as part of the role of network supervisor.

MAINFRAME TO LAN

Micro LANs offer two ways to communicate with a mainframe computer. First, each microcomputer on the LAN can be equipped with a terminal-emulation package. The micros can then set up direct sessions with the mainframe when necessary and use the LAN for intradepartmental communications. This solution is extremely costly. Not only must each micro get its own emulation hardware and software; each must also be supplied with a dedicated line to the communications controller and its own controller port. In general, the only time that networked micros should be given direct lines to the mainframe is when heavy use warrants the dedicated connection.

Usually, it is preferable to use the second approach, that of installing a mainframe communications gateway on the LAN (see figure 15–2). Any microcomputer on the LAN can establish

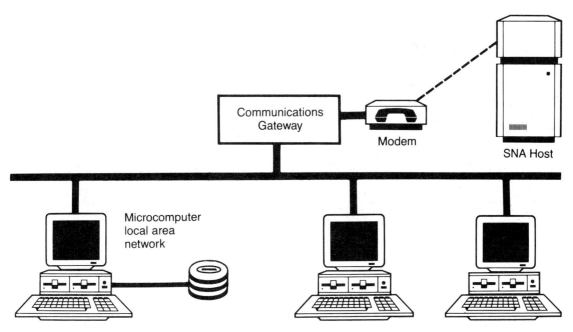

FIGURE 15–2: *LAN users can access the mainframe through an intelligent device called a* gateway. *The gateway converts mainframe and micro protocols so that information can pass between the two environments.*

a mainframe session by going through the gateway. The benefit of the gateway approach is that micros can share a single emulator and cable. In addition, the gateway replaces the communications controller and its associated costs.

Another advantage of the gateway is that it partially isolates the micro system from the terminal network. A microcomputer doing file transfer can drain communications resources and severely degrade the system's overall performance. The effect may be particularly noticeable at data entry terminals. When micros are attached to the mainframe through a gateway, the physical restrictions of the gateway and its single channel to the mainframe limit the impact of the micros on the remainder of the communications network. Usually this forces micro users to be more economical in their use of the mainframe, reducing the number and duration of sessions and the size of file transfers.

LOCAL AREA NETWORK OR MINICOMPUTER?

Architecturally, a LAN resembles a minicomputer system. Both systems permit the sharing of a central storage facility by connected workstations. The primary difference between the two systems is that a minicomputer system is designed to support dumb terminals, whereas a LAN is designed to support intelligent microcomputers. Microcomputers can attach to a minicomputer system, but they must do so by emulating a dumb terminal.

In a minicomputer system, all of the processing is performed by the minicomputer. On a LAN, the server handles only specific processing tasks, disk management (disk input/output), and communications. The applications processing on a LAN is performed at the individual workstations. To use the micro's processing capability with a minicomputer, you must download data to the micro and take them off-line for local processing. In multiuser applications, such as database management systems, this is not possible; the micro must remain on-line with the mini in order to ensure data integrity.

Designed for distributed processing, LAN operating systems use a set of software tools to synchronize multiuser accesses. Even though the processing is done at the workstation, data integrity is maintained. In part, this means that LANs are less expensive to build, because each added micro workstation brings its own processing power. To add processing power to a minicomputer network, you must usually buy another minicomputer.

Dependability is also less expensive to guarantee on a LAN. If a server malfunctions, most LANs permit another microcomputer to take over the server duties by attaching to the central hard disk and running the file-server software. To get the same dependability on a minicomputer network you must purchase a back-up mini.

An even more significant drawback to minicomputer systems is that a minicomputer-to-micro link must be established. All of the link problems discussed throughout this book must be solved, including application-format translation as you go from one environment to the other. In a LAN, the microcomputer environment prevails throughout. People need learn only one software package for each application, and they can use the easy-to-use microcomputer software.

SELECTING A LAN

Although LANs possess many common capabilities, the ways they achieve these capabilities vary considerably. The major characteristics of LANs include media, transmission method, topology, access scheme, and speed.

Media refers to the transmission media, or cables, used to connect the LAN hardware. Twisted-pair cables are the least expensive medium. They are suitable for smaller LANs with maximum bit rates in the 1-to-2 Mbs range. Coaxial cables are more expensive, but they support faster speeds and greater distances. Fiber-optic cables are the newest of the transmission media. This technology is still in the developmental stage and is costly; however, it supports very high transmission rates and will probably become the favored medium for large LANs.

Two transmission methods are in common use: baseband and broadband. Baseband uses the digital transmission as it comes from the computer without modification. Broadband converts the digital signal to a radio frequency (RF) signal, which is then transmitted onto the cable. Broadband requires special RF modems.

There are many topologies, or physical-layout schemes, used on LANs. The names of these topologies — stars, rings, and linear buses — suggest the configurations. Generally, the only reason to use one topology rather than another is cost for a particular installation. Some topologies may require more wire, but even that difference may be minimal.

The access scheme of a LAN is the method used to coordinate use of the shared media. Two workstations cannot transmit onto the same cable at the same time without causing a collision, in which case the messages must be retransmitted. Two access schemes dominate LANs: token-passing and CSMA-CD (carrier-sense multiple access with collision detection). In token-passing, a special control packet is passed from one station to another; a station must have possession of the packet before it can transmit. In CSMA-CD, a station wishing to transmit listens for a transmission; if none is detected, the station transmits. Because of its mathematically predictable means of passing network control, token-passing schemes are usually required in process-control systems, such as those common in factory robotics. Otherwise, there is little perceptible difference between the two schemes.

The speed of the LAN, when measured as raw bit rate, has little significance. Unfortunately, the raw bit rate is the only speed figure supplied by most LAN manufacturers. The real speed, which might be described variously as performance, response time, or throughput, is determined by the design of the network interface card and by the efficiency of the network operating system software. If a large LAN is planned, speed is a critical factor. The only satisfactory way to measure speed is to simulate an actual installation, using the same software and, ideally, the same number of workstations.

SUMMARY

LANS are high-speed communications networks that support microcomputers, allowing users to share peripherals and information and to communicate by means of electronic mail. An important function of the LAN is to bring isolated microcomputers and their users back into the organization. LANs encourage cooperation among micro users, while reducing duplication of work.

LANs started out as primitive systems that permitted people to share a hard disk. Early LANs had no mechanisms to handle concurrent users or information sharing. As microcomputer applications grew in power and sophistication, so did LANs. Modern LANs have become the ideal network for supporting attached microcomputers in a distributed processing environment.

16. IBM's Office Information Plan

IBM has developed a set of system-integration plans to cover most aspects of information processing. The overall goal is to permit information to flow from one hardware environment to another and from one application to another. Many system-integration plans have been developed by vendors, but probably none of the others will have the impact of those proposed by IBM. IBM's plans illustrate the direction of information processing. They are of particular interest to organizations using IBM mainframes and minis because of the near necessity of adopting IBM's strategy.

IBM'S OFFICE INFORMATION ARCHITECTURES

IBM's office information architectures are specifications for the dissemination and management of information in a system network. In this sense, a system network represents the collection of interconnected IBM systems and communications. The architectures define both the form of the information transmitted through the network and the rules governing the use of the information among the systems of the network.

Physically, a network is a combination of interconnected equipment and programs used for moving information between points at which it may be generated, processed, stored, and used.

From the viewpoint of its users, a network is a collection of services — in the case of an office system network, services useful in creating, revising, distributing, filing, and retrieving information.

Office systems may differ in several ways, for each offers different capabilites and answers the needs of different users. The thread that ties the systems together is telecommunications and information interchange. The goal is to let these dissimilar office systems communicate easily with one another in a universally understood manner.

What is needed is a uniform structure for information that is interchanged between office systems. This structure must have an encoding scheme that is designed to convey any document, regardless of its content, from one kind of office system to another and to communicate the intent of the person who creates or sends a document as to how it is to be processed.

The encoding scheme must also be flexible and extendible to allow it to accommodate new requirements as they arise. Rules must also be established to ensure that the various office systems interpret documents uniformly and act upon them in a consistent manner.

IBM meets the challenge of information interchange between office systems through a combination of methods, Document Content Architecture (DCA), Document Interchange Architecture (DIA), Systems Network Architecture (SNA), and Distributed Office Support System (DISOSS).

DCA

DCA describes the form and meaning of the content of a document that office systems can interchange through a network. The text of a document can be in revisable or final form. The content of a document whose text is in revisable form may be modified by each person to whom it is distributed or by whom it is obtained from a library. Conversely, a document whose text is in final form is intended for presentation on a printer or display screen rather than for subsequent modification.

Revisable-form-text DCA specifies how IBM office systems interchange documents that are in revisable form. This architecture defines the structure of the data streams that represent revisable-form-text documents within the office system or network. Besides the text of a document, a data stream includes fields containing general formatting specifications for the entire document or parts of it. The architecture also specifies the structure of the formatting control codes and text within revisable-form-text documents and prescribes how office systems must interpret them.

Final-form-text DCA specifies how IBM office systems interchange formatted text documents. Like revisable-form-text DCA, this DCA prescribes the structure of the data streams that represent documents within the office system or network. Unlike the revisable-form-text data stream, however, the final-form-text data stream does not include formatting specifications. The process of transforming text from revisable form to final form has converted the formatting specifications into control codes and generated text. The final-form-text data stream therefore contains the original text of the document, interspersed with the generated text, and control codes that cause the output device to print or display the document in the required format.

DIA

DIA defines how documents and requests for document distribution and processing functions are to be communicated through an office system network. DIA specifies the rules and data structures that establish the discipline for unambiguous interchange of documents and other information between office systems.

SNA

SNA (see figure 16–1) has been described by IBM as the strategic communications protocol of the future. Prior to SNA (and sometimes after SNA), IBM used bisynchronous communications to communicate from host to workstation and from host to host. Most large organizations with IBM mainframes will have a large installed base of bisync devices (for example, 3278 terminals). Because of the complexities of today's data requirements, however, SNA is moving to the forefront.

SNA is particularly strong in the area of packet-naming con-

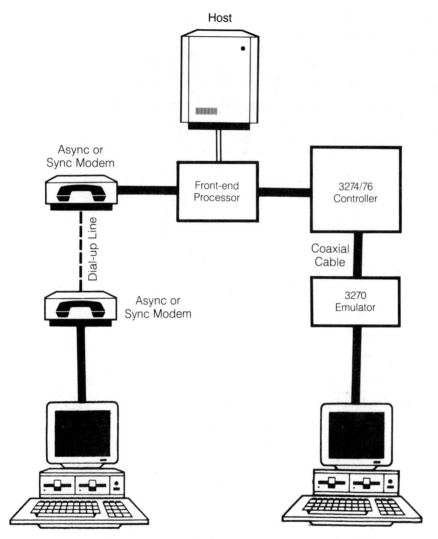

Host

Async or
Sync Modem

Front-end
Processor

3274/76
Controller

Dial-up Line

Async or
Sync Modem

Coaxial
Cable

3270
Emulator

FIGURE 16–1: *SNA
communications can
be accomplished
through synchronous
dial-up lines or dedi-
cated coaxial cable.
Both techniques sup-
port the same
functionality.*

ventions. In essence, all devices in a SNA network are logically
addressable. This addressing or naming allows communications
to take place across the entire network. For organizations that
may be spread across the U.S., or the world for that matter, SNA
provides a means of transparent addressing across all devices.
This means, for example, that an individual in New York could
talk to a computer in London and never know that she was com-

municating through five different SNA networks.

IBM has continued to improve on the SNA approach since its introduction in 1978. In the early stages, SNA had two major limitations, which concerned many system integrators. First, the number of nodes, known as *physical units* (PUs), that could be connected to one SNA network, was limited. (A PU is usually a mainframe or a front-end communications processor.) Second, there was also a limit on the number of workstations, known as *logical units*, or LUs, that could be attached to a network.

The initial limitations of SNA have been addressed by the System Network Interconnection (SNI) enhancement. SNI has two main components: first, it provides a means of interconnecting multiple, independent SNA networks. This cross-connection capability allows workstations (LUs) on one network to access applications on another SNA network. Second, SNI allows an organization to break down a larger network into smaller, more efficient, systems. Because an SNA/SNI network can be split into subnets, the addressing limitations of the previous SNA are reduced. For example, if an SNA network is approaching address capacity, breaking the network into three smaller SNA networks would triple the address potential of the network as a whole.

In general, IBM's SNA communications protocol approach will offer the needed flexibility to address the complex networks of the future. Large-scale networks will be a driving force in the computer/communications industries into the 1990s. Companies with large installed bases of IBM equipment should strategically plan for the use of SNA.

DISOSS

DISOSS is primarily a high-level document exchange and control application. In the overall IBM strategy for interconnecting systems, DISOSS is used to coordinate actions at the mainframe level. The history of DISOSS is unusual. The program runs under the MVS operating system of IBM mainframes. A competitive product, also from IBM, is called Professional Office System (PROFS) and is much like DISOSS.

Two major differences exist between the two products. First, PROFS runs under a different operating system, known as VM.

The second difference is that PROFS is rich in features but architecturally poor, if you examine the complete IBM information-processing strategy. Although DISOSS has few features compared to PROFS, it provides the architecture toward which the IBM strategy is directed. Because of its structure, IBM has chosen to move forward with DISOSS.

Several feature enhancements have been targeted for DISOSS as plans are implemented across major IBM product lines. The combination of DISOSS and SNA will serve as a foundation for future IBM system strategy.

PERSONAL SERVICES

In late 1984, IBM introduced another strategic direction for interconnecting its computer systems. Personal Services was introduced to provide a standard user interface and functionality across a variety of IBM systems.

Personal Services/370

Personal Services/370 (PS/370) provides distributed office support systems (DISOSS) capabilities at the mainframe level. In effect, PS/370 and DISOSS work hand in hand to provide electronic-office functionality to IBM workstations. Such capabilities as electronic mail, calendar management, and document-distribution are found in PS/370 and are provided in conjunction with DISOSS.

Personal Services/36

Personal Services/36 (PS/36) operates much as PS/370 does. As the name implies, PS/36 functions within the System 36 environment; through the use of the SNA Distribution Services (SNADS), it can also communicate with PS/370 running on a larger mainframe.

PS/36 is part of a total System 36 integrated office support plan. In conjunction with PS/36, DisplayWrite/36 is offered for word processing and Query/36 is provided for datafile manipulation. Much as PS/370 does, PS/36 offers advanced office solutions such as electronic document distribution, calendar management, directory support, and group processing. PS/36 operates as a type of controlling software environment; it manages all document transmission on a local System/36, as well as documents sent and received from mainframes running PS/370 or other System/36 machines.

Personal Services/PC

IBM has also developed a workstation version of Personal Services, known as Personal Services/PC (PS/PC). PS/PC serves as a user interface to advanced versions of Personal Services that run on larger processors, such as the System/36 and the IBM mainframes. PS/PC interacts with DISOSS functions running on a host computer. Because the mainframe is not going to disappear, IBM continues to tie many functions and capabilities to a central processor of some type, whether it be a mainframe or a departmental processor.

For the most part, PS/PC is used to send and receive messages, documents, and personal-services files from other PS systems. One advantage of PS/PC is that many operations can be performed on an unattended personal computer, if the PS/PC program is left running on that computer. PS/PC can communicate with PS/370 in two modes — through asynchronous dial-up lines or through 3278 emulation products.

SUMMARY

IBM's systems and communications strategies often become industry standards. IBM has openly endorsed SNA, DISOSS, DCA, DIA, and Personal Services as overall strategic products. For companies that have or expect to have installed bases of IBM equipment, these standards should be part of system planning. Furthermore, for environments with mixed vendor equipment, including some IBM machines, these standards should be followed as closely as possible.

17. Security

WHEN asked about the security provisions of his program, a software developer answers, "Why would you want passwords and other protections on a microcomputer? Security mechanisms serve only to make the micro less accessible. The microcomputer should be as available as a telephone."

The head of a university's computing services reacts toward security in much the same way: "We have no special security provisions for our communications network. None of the data on our network needs protection."

Resistance to security is common among computer managers and users. Security is inconvenient and costly. As the microcomputer becomes more integrated in organizational computing, however, the need for good security is inevitable. Many micro users were shocked when manufacturers started equipping their micros with locks and keys. However, it established the point that valuable data are accessible through the microcomputer and that ways must be found to protect those data.

DATA INTEGRITY AND SECURITY

Security and data integrity are often placed together under a broad category called "protecting your data." Actually, though, the problems and solutions in data protection are easier to understand if security and integrity are examined as two separate subjects.

Data-integrity measures, which will be discussed in chapter 18, are protections against unintentional threats. Careless data handling and transmission/translation errors are examples of data-integrity problems. Data security, on the other hand, is the system used to protect data from intentional threats, such as theft and vandalism. Electronic transmission and storage of data have made data highly vulnerable to misuse of this type.

The microcomputer is a convenient and powerful tool for so-called white-collar crime. Sometimes the crimes involve the direct theft of cash. Once protection mechanisms are breached, accounts and pay records can be altered to enrich the criminal. The micro, with its disk storage system, is used in industrial espionage, in which company records are taken to be sold to competitors.

Micros have also helped spawn a new breed of amateur criminal, the computer hacker who challenges security systems just to see if they can be beaten. In the same vein, "software piracy" has become yet another security threat. Although copying a disk seldom seems like a real crime to the person doing the copying, it may lead to multimillion-dollar law suits filed against the "pirate's" employers.

PLANNING FOR SECURITY

Many security devices and procedures are available. The micro marketplace offers the products to build a labyrinth of locks, screens, and encryptors that can defend against anything up to and including James Bond and nuclear attack. What you must determine is how far you wish to go toward total security. Security makes authorized access more difficult and time-consuming. Navigating through ID checks and passwords can be a slow, frustrating experience.

If an organization could keep all of its data in one place and never let anyone in to use or even read them, the data would be "secure." Because that would defeat the purpose of having the data, however, it is not a viable option. Managing data in an organization means reconciling two incompatible goals. People want their workstations and data to be convenient and accessible, yet they want their data safe and secure. Stated another way, security is a matter of compromises with two major variables: accessibility and security. The greater the security, the lower the accessibility (see figure 17–1).

Before the protection devices and stratagems can be discussed, the threats against which they are designed to protect must be examined. In addition, some kind of price tag must be put on potential losses. Choosing a security system is like purchasing any other form of insurance: the cost of the insurance shouldn't exceed the value of whatever you're insuring.

Designing a practical security system involves evaluating the potential threat and formulating an appropriate level of protection. The steps in this process are listed below:

1. Identify micro workstation capabilities.
2. Categorize the data accessible to the micro.
3. Evaluate (in dollars) the potential threat.
4. List available security measures.
5. Build an appropriate security system as measured against the potential threat.

IDENTIFYING MICRO CAPABILITIES

Microcomputers can be placed in two general categories: stand-alone and networked. A stand-alone microcomputer that is not part of a communications network poses no threat to the central database. This removes a primary area of concern, but it doesn't mean that the micro can be ignored in terms of security. Microcomputer data, stored on a hard disk or floppy disk, should be properly protected. This is the responsibility of the individual and is no different from safeguarding documents. More directly related to the micro is the problem of software piracy. With a stand-alone micro configured with floppy disk drives, applications software can be illegally copied.

The networked microcomputer has the potential to use any resources attached to the network. In a fully distributed system,

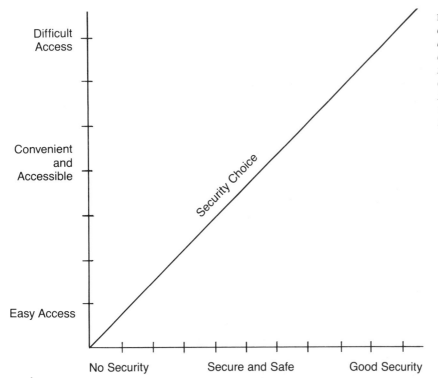

FIGURE 17–1: *Good security usually reduces ease of access to the computer. Managers must weigh the trade-offs between convenience and security when implementing a specific system.*

workstations are difficult to protect physically from unauthorized use. Cables are long and usually offer many opportunities for tapping. Distributed dial-up networks, which use public telephone lines, are open to attack by anyone with a microcomputer and a modem. Any micro equipped with local storage capability can capture data. This makes data not only accessible but also portable.

To summarize, only a few micro characteristics pertain to security. On a security checklist, machines might be divided into four groups: stand alone micros, networked micros, micros with no removable local storage, and micros with removable local storage.

CATEGORIZING DATA AND EVALUATING THE THREAT

The threat to data must be evaluated before a rational plan can be designed. Evaluation, in this case, means considering what data are accessible by micros and then placing a value on those data.

Data theft is a relatively new concept. Until just a few years ago, data theft or vandalism was rare. Most of our data was stored in bulky file cabinets. Unless you were a defense contractor or a bank, it was unlikely that anyone would accept the risk of stealing your data. Other targets, such as merchandise and office equipment, were more convenient and easier to sell. Magnetic storage systems changed all that. Now, the business plans and records of a medium-sized company can be stored on a single tape cartridge that will slip into a coat pocket. A large company without good security could have all of its data seriously damaged in minutes.

Data processing organizations usually recognize the value of data and take precautions to protect it. With the introduction of micros, however, the control of valuable data is steadily shifting from central locations to distributed sites. A department or even an individual at a remote site may have access to large amounts of highly sensitive data.

People responsible for the data must be concerned with vandalism as much as they are with outright theft. To be at risk, data need not even be marketable. An accountant of a small company arrived at work one morning to find that all of the company's accounts-receivable records had been erased from their storage area on a hard disk. Although the vandal probably received no monetary gain, the company's loss was substantial.

The problems of protecting data vary with the type of data. Three general types of losses can be identified: loss of secrecy, loss of information, and alteration of information. Classifying data according to the potential type of loss is imperative in planning a protection scheme. For example, it would cause no damage if an in-depth analysis of market conditions were destroyed by a vandal (loss of information). However, if the analysis were acquired by a competitor (loss of secrecy), the damage might be costly. Therefore, denial of unauthorized access is the only suitable protection against loss of secrecy.

Accounts receivable may be kept secret for privacy reasons, but loss of secrecy would probably not cause a financial loss. Erasure of the accounts receivable by vandals, however, would result in lost revenue. In this case, a good back-up procedure should be the primary security measure.

A company would lose money through alteration of information if someone gave himself a raise or transferred funds to a personal account. Here denial of unauthorized access and some means of auditing record changes are called for.

Once data have been classified, they should be assigned a monetary value. This is often one of the most difficult steps in security planning. If loss of the data would require its recreation, such a cost should be easily determined. If a theft of data would cause loss of prestige or tougher competition, you may only be able to estimate its dollar value. To some extent you can avoid precise evaluation by assigning security codes. "Top secret" would mean that the loss could jeopardize the future of the company. "Secret" would mean that the loss could cause serious damage. "Confidential" would mean that the loss could cause only minor damage.

LISTING POSSIBLE SECURITY MEASURES

The third step in planning for micro security is to list the possible options. Micro security can involve many different types of systems and procedures. You can organize these into three categories: system security, physical security, and administrative security.

System Security

System security includes all of the security features built into the communications network. Passwords and user profiles are common examples. System security could also include data encryption and call-screening devices. All of these various features are designed to work automatically — that is, they don't depend on human intervention.

In a micro-to-mainframe network, the most important security measure is the log-in procedure. It is included as part of system security because the mechanism is entailed in the system. Once it is implemented, the log-in procedure is fully automated. The log-in system is a gateway between your keyboard and mainframe data. The first part of the system requires you to present a log-in name, which is usually your actual name, your nickname, or your name and initial.

If the system identifies you as an authorized user, it will next ask for a password. The system matches passwords to log-in names; each name has been assigned its own unique password. To be effective, passwords must be secret. One way the system can help maintain this secrecy is by not "echoing" a typed password to the display. When you respond to the request for a password, your response won't show up on the screen where someone else could read it.

A good password system restricts the number of attempts for entering a valid password. After receiving three invalid passwords, for example, the system will disallow the log-in name and notify a supervisor. Such a limit on log-in attempts is crucial when dealing with microcomputers. The intelligent micro is capable of being programmed to try all alphanumeric combinations until the valid password is found. The search may take just minutes and can be prevented only by limiting the number of log-in attempts. (Use of passwords will be discussed more under adminstrative security.)

Once a successful log-in is completed, you can make requests through the network. When you request specific data, a combination of system and application software will compare your log-in name to a *user profile*, which defines the areas to which you are authorized access.

REMOTE ACCESS SECURITY   When a network supports dial-up communications, the security challenge increases. Physical security measures are nullified because physical access isn't required for dial-up access. Responsibility for security rests almost exclusively with system security (see figure 17–2).

A special screening device can be added to the system to reduce the threat. A programmable box is placed between the incoming line and the mainframe. The box may require an access code before permitting the caller to log-in. If the access code is invalid, the box can be programmed to deny additional attempts, sound or display alarms, and initiate call tracing.

Some dial-up screening devices additionally use a call-back procedure. After the caller supplies a code, he disconnects. The

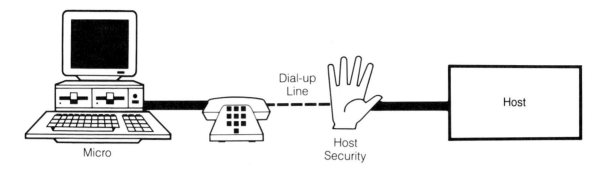

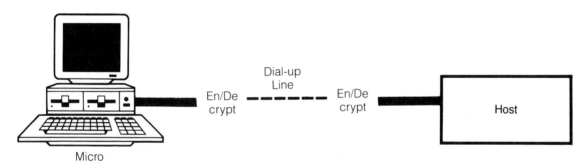

screening device then calls a telephone number matching the personal code it received. Thus, only registered sites can log-in to the network.

DATA ENCRYPTION SYSTEMS   Any time a message is transmitted, it is vulnerable to being intercepted. People usually think of eavesdropping on radio traffic, but cable transmissions can also become targets. Cables can be tapped, or signal radiation emitted from the cable can be monitored without a physical tap.

Authorized micro workstations can be a problem, too. Intelligent microcomputers don't require dedicated cables. Messages can be affixed with an address and broadcast through a shared cable, the micro responding to messages bearing its address. It is not difficult for a technician to circumvent the addressing

FIGURE 17–2: *When a computer system can be accessed through telephone lines, security measures must be taken to protect against unauthorized access. Two ways to protect the system are call-back mechanisms and data encryption.*

scheme and monitor any messages on the cable. To prevent this kind of unauthorized access, you can use a number of data-encryption systems. Encryption is the process of systematically altering data so that it is unreadable until the process is reversed (decryption).

Encryption is usually based on a mathematical algorithm. Again, because of its intelligence, the microcomputer is an ideal tool to attack the system. However, designers now calculate the number of computations required in a random-search attack. They can select numbers so large that successfully breaking the code is computationally infeasible. Based on the length of time needed to break the code, encryption schemes are labeled as meeting various standards. A simple scheme may provide what is known as *data privacy*. This is adequate for normal office security, but insufficient for high-security traffic, such as banking transactions.

Banks usually adopt an encryption algorithm that meets a federally defined minimum for encryption called DES (Data Encryption Standard). When extremely sophisticated attacks might be expected, security experts may feel that DES is insufficient and may demand even more complex systems.

ACTIVITY MONITORING   Regardless of the quality of your access security, unauthorized penetration always remains possible. Additionally, people may make improper use of data to which they have authorized access. Database software should provide some means of monitoring when data is manipulated and by whom. These monitoring systems, called audit trails, are often considered only as accounting mechanisms that help in the billing of resource use. They can also be of invaluable aid, however, in discouraging tampering and in tracing data misuse.

SOLVING THE LOCAL STORAGE PROBLEM   Data theft and software piracy are security problems that are especially related to the microcomputer. Both of these problems can be virtually eliminated through the use of diskless micros, microcomputers without disk drives.

Implementing diskless micros requires a local area network. The program necessary to start the micro workstation is supplied in firmware, which is plugged into the micro. As soon as the micro is turned on, the firmware program makes the connection to a central hard disk. You can then load applications stored on the hard disk and use the disk's data-file areas.

Physical Security

Physical security is an external mechanism that bars access. In fact, bars can be a part of physical security, along with locks, alarms, and guards. During normal office hours, personal recognition is a functional method of physical security. You recognize people who are authorized to be sitting at a micro workstation in your office. After hours, locks and alarms can take over.

One method of physical security that is often overlooked is network containment. Extremely sensitive data should be kept on a separate network, and it should be given its own dedicated host. When the sensitive-data network is confined to a single floor of a building, security can be high. If the sensitive-data network must be tied into the general communications system, the connection should be through a gateway or bridge. This retains the separate network environment, while permitting internetwork communications. Normal, intranetwork traffic is not broadcast across a gateway and thus cannot be intercepted.

Administrative Security

Administrative security consists of the procedures that are set up to protect the system. Classification codes (secret, confidential, etc.) are part of administrative security. So are procedural directives, such as "Lock keyboards when not in use" and "Don't divulge passwords to colleagues."

Administrative security is inexpensive, adaptable, and effective. The essential keys to its success are user awareness and cooperation. Passwords are a good example of the importance of user cooperation. If people freely divulge passwords, the entire log-in procedure becomes corrupted and ineffective.

The tools of administrative security are procedures and guidelines, password assignment, security education, and back-ups.

PROCEDURES AND GUIDELINES   Part of the process of building a mainframe-micro security system involves identifying workstation capabilities and classifying accessible data. These are ongoing functions that must be addressed as part of administrative security. User profiles are implemented as part of the system (system security), but they must be maintained as a function of administrative security.

PASSWORD ASSIGNMENT   Passwords should be assigned by a supervisor, using arbitrary words. When people are allowed to set their own passwords, they usually select words that are easy to remember, such as their title or their spouse's or child's name. This kind of password can often be guessed in a few attempts.

Supervisors should change passwords on a regular basis. As a rule, the longer passwords are retained the less secret they become. Changing passwords also provides an opportunity to stress the need for security among employees. If a company goes to the trouble of changing passwords, employees tend to take security more seriously.

SECURITY EDUCATION   DP departments can set up elaborate and effective security schemes, but they can only be marginally effective without the participation of the people using the data. A good education program can remind people frequently of the value of the data with which they work and point out the need for conscientiously following security procedures.

BACK-UPS   Most mainframe systems have excellent back-up equipment and procedures. With microcomputers at the departmental and individual levels, however, back-ups may be largely ignored. All critical data should be copied, and the copy should be retained in a location separate from the primary storage. The key factor in designing good back-up systems is simplicity. Back-up devices can be programmed to copy all new or modifed files at the end of the regular workday. Some systems may require no human intervention other than the pressing of a button and the changing of tapes.

BUILDING A SECURITY SYSTEM

The fifth and final step in securing data is bringing the pieces of the analysis together and building the security system. A good security system is built of many components, which should be assembled to handle many contingencies. Physical security is never 100-percent impenetrable, system security will inevitably have flaws, and administrative security cannot be perfect because people will occasionally become lax. Together, however, the various types of security can identify and/or nullify deficiencies in one another to produce a secure environment.

Good security is multilayered. That is, in security terms, two locks are better than one. When you are selecting security components, it's important to understand that no single device or procedure is totally secure. Security is really a strategy to make unauthorized access difficult, costly, and time-consuming.

SUMMARY

In the first two steps of security analysis, you define the risk of problems based on the capability of the workstations and on the type of data available to those workstations. These steps give you an indication of where your system is vulnerable. The third step calls for placing a dollar value on potential losses. This provides you with a value to match against the cost of security measures. That value, along with an estimate of frequency of occurrence, should help you decide how much to spend on security. (Police departments and industry groups can often supply information on the frequency of thefts and vandalism.) In the fourth step, you look at the security measures available to you. Finally, in the fifth step, you put these pieces together and develop an appropriate security system.

This chapter has focused on the ways to secure a mainframe-micro system, but the greater problem is to get people to initiate security measures in the first place. Security is costly and offers no tangible benefit other than the knowledge that "something bad is not happening." Because of this, security is often difficult for management to enthusiastically fund and support.

18. Data Integrity

IN the game Gossip, a story is retold from one person to another. The object of the game is to relay the story as accurately as possible. After half a dozen people have received and relayed the story, however, all of its details usually have been materially changed. Gossip is not a win-or-lose game, just an example (in this case, an amusing one) of how human beings unwittingly alter information.

If businesses handled information with the same precision, it would be far from amusing — it would be catastrophic. Business systems cannot exist with unreliable data. In traditional computing, the reliability of data, referred to as *data integrity*, is a fundamental ingredient. Data that are kept on the mainframe system and processed with mainframe software are protected by programming practices and procedures developed over several decades.

With the integration of the microcomputer into corporate computing, data integrity is no longer assured by conventional means. The microcomputer, more than any other computing device, is an extension of its operator. This is what makes the micro attractive to the user. Without special safeguards, however, the microcomputer is an open door to data misuse.

The tendency among many managers is to take a bureaucratic

approach to eliminating poor data integrity on micros. Companies can require the use of micro software that includes mainframe-type data integrity features, such as entry validation. This is not normally practiced at the micro level.

Files transfer — the moving of files between a micro and a mainframe — is often considered a threat to data integrity. To safeguard such transfers, many companies permit the downloading of files from the mainframe to the micro but prohibit uploading from the micro to the mainframe environment. Some companies have gone so far as to prohibit any file transfers between the microcomputer and the mainframe.

Is rigid DP department control necessary for microcomputers? Do microcomputers by their nature pose high risks to corporate data? These questions deserve examination.

DATA INTEGRITY AT THE MICRO

The microcomputer itself is not an unreliable handler of data. Data at the micro are not subject to higher risks than those found generally within a computing system. As both a computer and a workstation, however, the micro does require some modification of traditional procedures.

Before deciding upon the best approach to protect data at the micro, you should carefully consider the micro environment. In many cases, forcing data processing procedures on microcomputer users may not be appropriate. Most microcomputers are personal computers used by an individual as a tool to do a job. The user is totally responsible for the data, whether the data are stored on a floppy disk or a mainframe time-sharing system. In a time-sharing situation, prohibiting or restricting transfers of data will not guarantee data integrity. The competence of the worker is the only assurance that the data is valid.

A better way to improve data integrity at the microcomputer begins with educating micro users about the system and showing them how the reliability of data is threatened and how to protect data. In a micro system, the primary threat to data integrity is the result of multiple copies of data. Because micros have their own processing capability, data files can be copied into the micro system and altered. As soon as the data are altered, there is one version of the data at the source (perhaps the mainframe database) and another version at the microcomputer.

The problem of multiple copies is most easily understood in an inventory system. The central database says that the company has 120 brown chairs. A person on a microcomputer checks current inventory (120 chairs) and then sells 50 of those chairs. At that moment, the inventory on the central database still says 120 chairs are available, on the salesperson's computer, however, the inventory record says 70 chairs are in stock (see figure 18–1).

Multiple copies also can cause problems with written reports. A junior executive writes a report, keeps the original, and sends a copy on disk to the boss. The boss makes a few changes using his word processor and returns the disk. It would be easy at this point to lose track of which is the original and which is the corrected version. In some situations, forwarding the wrong version could have serious consequences.

The process of eliminating conflicting versions of the same data is know as *synchronization*. Because of the processing capability of the micro, the micro user must know what synchronization is and must support DP efforts to reduce multiple versions of data.

A fundamental way to reduce the problem is to label data, whether it is stored magnetically or printed out. Organizations should consider methods for distinguishing mainframe-generated data from microcomputer data. This could be done by using specially colored paper to distinguish mainframe reports from those developed at the micro. Only certain people in the company should have authorization to use the "mainframe" paper. Then, when a manager makes a data-integrity audit, the mainframe data can be considered valid. Valid data can be compared to microcomputer data. Mainframe paper would be put only on certain printers and would be strictly controlled by the computer operations staff that runs all of the peripheral equipment.

On magnetic media, files should be renamed as soon as they are modified. The file name and report heading should indicate that the data have been modified and should identify who made the modification and when it was made.

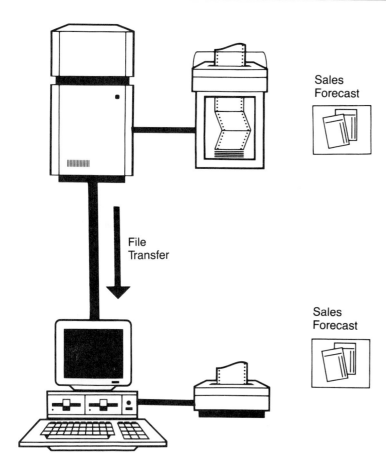

FIGURE 18–1: *A frequent problem in mainframe-micro integration occurs when data is copied from one environment to another. Here, sales forecasts were generated at both the mainframe and the micro using the same data; it can be difficult to determine which of these versions is accurate.*

Sales Forecast

File Transfer

Sales Forecast

When several people begin to modify shared data, synchronization becomes more difficult to manage. In production systems, in which the central database is being updated, elaborate procedures are used to assure proper updating. Major production systems filter data before they allow data to come in. Whether that data comes from a micro, a terminal, or a batch transfer from a time-sharing system, production systems must have a significant amount of protection to synchronize data and make sure data has not been damaged. The protection includes various tests of the data.

For on-line data entry, applications software must verify the data as they are entered. If an operator tries to enter the wrong data, such as entering the name of a company where the address should go, the software will disallow the entry and notify the operator. Off-line processing and batch uploading require the same kind of control. For example, a microcomputer user could not download mainframe data, process them off-line, and then upload them directly into the central database. Once the data are taken off-line, out of a secure environment, they can no longer be considered in synchronization with the mainframe data. There is always the possibility that the microcomputer user will bring the data down, make no changes, and whatever he prints out will be exactly the same as the mainframe data. Because the manager has no control over that, however, it must be assumed that as soon as the data leave the mainframe environment and enter a microcomputer, the synchronization is gone.

Microcomputers can emulate terminals. Because terminals cannot capture and then manipulate data, all of the on-line data-integrity protections remain in place. Terminal-emulation packages, however, typically permit a micro user to switch easily from terminal mode to microcomputer mode. They also support some type of file-capture facility to let users pull down data and manipulate them off-line. In general, this mode-switching is so simple that it cannot be prevented; thus, even emulator-equipped micros cannot be treated as terminals where sensitive data is concerned.

Today, on-line technology is intermixed with the micro's off-line processing and batch-entry method. The microcomputer takes data off-line and performs stand-alone manipulation. The critical factor is that the validation of information in this process is in the users' hands, not those of the central data processing department.

The upload capability of a micro enables data created on a distributed personal computer system to be moved to a central business database. Uploading significantly increases the risk of invalid data, because integrity controls are often unavailable. Uploaded data can taint the corporate database on which business decisions are dependent. The security and validation of data when micros are allowed to upload should be handled by the mainframe; doing so allows the integrity of the information to be controlled. Normally, after files are modified off-line by a mi-

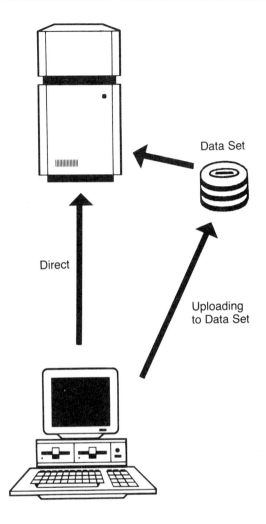

FIGURE 18–2: *One way to control uploading from the mainframe to the micro is to use an intermediate dataset. When a dataset is used, the data processing department can check and verify data before it is stored in the main database or file.*

Data Set

Direct

Uploading
to Data Set

crocomputer, they should be uploaded to a special area of mainframe storage. The DP department can then check the source and the accuracy of the data before merging them into the central database.

One of the data-integrity options is to use scheduled processing, in which technique data from a micro are not automatically used to update the mainframe database. Instead, data are processed in a batch mode and sent to a mainframe dataset, or temporary file (see figure 18–2). A computer program will automatically load and process these intermediate dataset names. Security codes or other identifiers can be used to make sure that valid datasets are being processed.

For example, say that you have a file with ten records. You could assign security codes to individuals such that the first record in a file would have a certain security code. When a program pulls in that dataset, the security code is noted and the program continues to process the file. If the code is not in the file, the program disregards the file.

The reason for using an embedded security code is as follows: suppose the code is based only on a file name. Someone could learn the name of the dataset required to get the data updated; that would not be not difficult, because a copy of the program might be less than thoroughly secured. Using that name, that person might thwart the security scheme. If the code is embedded into the file and is changed randomly, however, the security is much greater.

Uploading typically requires no special host software. Data processed and uploaded from microcomputers will use the already available editor on a mainframe. This editor is normally accessed via a terminal keyboard. The micro uploading process is exactly the same as typing, except that the pace is faster. Because the process requires no host code, the micro user automatically has the capability of doing a certain amount of uploading. So although host software is not required, a host editor is required to control the process.

The systems put in place to control this access must consider capabilites that were not available before the micro. Editors were written with dumb terminals in mind. The micro is a new technology and requires its own set of controls. In other words, even though uploading requires no host code, the new micro-mainframe environment may require optimizing of mainframe hardware and software interfaces.

SHARING DATA AT THE MICRO LEVEL

The methods and procedures for synchronization within a production system are the responsibility of the data processing department. When data are stored in shared files at the micro level, however, the micro user is often responsible for the actual synchronization.

Local area networks (LANs) provide a means of connecting microcomputers so that the micros can communicate and share peripherals (see chapter 15). The LAN also permits information-sharing from shared files stored on a central hard disk. The primary problem with LANs has been that they often support information-sharing without providing automated data-integrity mechanisms. For example, user A can copy a file from the hard disk into his microcomputer. If the file can be shared, user B can get a copy of the same file. If user A stores the updated file and then user B stores his update, the LAN software may store user B's version on top of user A's version, destroying user A's work.

New LAN software is available that avoids this kind of synchronization problem, but many less sophisticated LAN software products are still sold and widely used. Furthermore, poor synchronization may be found not only on LANs but also on minicomputer systems. When any local system is installed at the micro level, users should carefully verify the system's synchronization capabilities before attempting to share information.

Departmental processors with linked-in microcomputers can also be used to help centralize and synchronize data for a group of micro users.

DATA MOVEMENT

Synchronization problems happen because of poor data-handling procedures or because of poor software design. Data integrity also can be threatened through some fault in the computer and communications system, either hardware or software. Data are often lost or damaged during movement from one system to another or from one format to another. The topic of how such problems occur and how they can be avoided are discussed elsewhere in this book. From the user's standpoint, the important thing is to be prepared for errors and to learn how to identify them.

User Awareness

By far the biggest problem with data integrity at the user level is caused by inattention. Computers seem to encourage an uncritical attitude: "The computer gave me the figure, so it must be correct." This can be a fatal assumption.

Users should look for clues to inaccurate data. Most software, for example, creates neat reports with straight columns. If a report is received in which the columns are out of line, it's likely that an error occurred in the data transmission. If the column is shifted four characters to the left, it's an indication that four characters may have been lost. Such pattern recognition can tell the user that something is wrong with the report. This is particularly helpful in validating graphs and spreadsheets. The problem might be in the logic on the mainframe, in the transmission, or in the translation from a mainframe to a micro format. The important thing is to recognize the signs of an error.

Usually the end user is using the microcomputer as an efficiency tool and already has a good intuitive feel for what is right and wrong. The end user is also the person who has the ultimate responsibility for the correctness of the data.

STORAGE AND BACK-UP

Magnetic storage systems offer a number of advantages, including rapid modification of data. Yet the ability to modify data rapidly has a drawback: data destruction can occur as quickly as data modification. Few micro users have escaped the horror that comes from erasing the wrong file, spilling coffee on a disk, or having a disk drive crash.

As more valuable data is placed at the micro, users must be made aware of the fragile nature of magnetic storage and of the best procedures for backing up their data. Practically, there is no way to avoid data losses; they can occur as the result of both mechanical and human error. A good back-up procedure can prevent such losses from being costly.

Whenever possible, users should be equipped with tape back-up devices that quickly copy hard-disk data onto removable tape cartridges. Critical data should be backed up regularly and the back-up should be stored away from the central site so that fire and other catastrophes cannot destroy the data.

ACCOUNTABILITY

So far, data integrity has been examined in three environments — the stand-alone/time-sharing environment, the DP production environment, and the shared-microcomputer environment. During the past 20 years, controls have been developed in traditional DP facilities to ensure that data are correct and complete. Other controls have been developed to ensure capability with business and process cycles. Few of these controls, however, have been transferred to the new microcomputer environment.

Overall data integrity in most companies is handled by the database administrator (DBA). The DBA is responsible for maintaining data integrity at the host level. Data integrity is a responsibility of all levels, even down to the level of the department and the end user.

It is most important to avoid implementing or permitting a communications network between micro and mainframe that could somehow circumvent the DBA. If uploading is done, it should go through the DBA's scrutiny.

For accountability, departments should assign an individual to become the police person of information in that department. This person maintains data integrity so that the manager who receives the data can rely on their accuracy. The "police person" should be a neutral party, not part of the accounting department or the finance department, and he should report to upper management. An outside person is desirable. In any case, someone must be accountable. An alternative would be to have individuals be responsible for any data they generate. People should be concerned with data integrity.

In the evolving computing environment, any department with one or two microcomputers must be tasked with maintaining data integrity. This creates the need for a Distributed Database Administrator who is subordinate to the mainframe DBA. Upper management must rigidly enforce the concept that the department is responsible for its information and for data flow-ing to the upper management. If the data are inaccurate, a manager could make misinformed decisions that jeopardize the department and possibly the company as a whole.

The DBA at the mainframe level should stay in contact with distributed DBAs to make sure that the procedures they are enforcing at the departmental level are consistent and work in conjunction with the controls and plans used at the mainframe level. The strategic plans of the DBA at the host level, in other words, should coincide with the plans and procedures of distributed DBAs at lower levels.

WHO'S RESPONSIBLE FOR THE DATA?

The most important idea here is that you are responsible for your own actions, whether or not you use a microcomputer. If you misuse the microcomputer and you don't watch what you do in the spreadsheet — putting your formulas in incorrectly, for example — your job may be on the line.

DP people are recognizing that the micro is an important part of the future of computing. They know that they must provide good data processing services to the microcomputer end user and that they are not going to be able to dictate the ways in which they provide those services. Large DP departments must remember that they are in business for the end user and not for themselves. DP must move back to a service-oriented business unit.

COSTS OF DATA INTEGRITY

The cost of data integrity is often difficult to justify — there's no visible, immediate return on an expenditure. Some costs must be associated with microcomputers, in addition to the more obvious hardware, software, and training. You must have a support staff. Someone must write procedures, guidelines, and documentation for microcomputer software. Additionally, someone must be appointed as a controlling force of information to make sure that audit trails, back-ups, and all other necessary procedures are followed at the micro level. These costs must be borne to ensure the success of microcomputers in the business world. The more distributed the computing environment becomes, the more such safeguards must be implemented.

SUMMARY

No micro-mainframe integration can or should be contemplated until the issue of data integrity is resolved. The microcomputer is not fundamentally a threat to data, but its misuse can be disastrous.

When data are brought down from the mainframe to the micro and stored on disk or in RAM, they can be modified in any way that the user wishes. The mainframe data-integrity safeguards are no longer in place. If the data are to be used in reports, they should be labeled as micro-generated to differentiate them from mainframe data.

Uploading data from the micro to the mainframe can be done in batch mode. To avoid corrupting the mainframe data, the uploading process should be conducted in stages. The data are first sent to an intermediate storage area in which they can be verified. Only after the verification should the micro data be moved into the mainframe database.

19. Management Planning

THE data processing organization is staffed with individuals to operate, program, and manage computer-related services. Over the years the DP organization has served as the keeper or custodian of data for companies. Typically, the data are representative of large systems, such as payroll, accounts receivable, and order entry. In addition to these major systems, DP organizations are increasingly responsible for developing systems that management can rely on to make decisions. In addition, as more and more requests flow into DP organizations, a backlog of incompleted work often develops. Largely because of the workload, DP organizations have developed a reputation for being unresponsive and for not giving management and end users what was needed.

In an attempt to improve their image and show a willingness to carry out management wishes, DP organizations began calling themselves management information systems (MIS) groups. The combination of a new identity, increased pressure, technological advances, and experience has done much to improve the overall effectiveness of MIS groups.

THE REDEFINING OF THE COMPUTER INDUSTRY

For today's MIS manager, the keys to success often center around determining when and how to implement, integrate, communicate with, and manage rapidly changing computing technologies. The computer industry has gone through several phases of redefinition. These evolutions have served to improve efficiency, reduce cost, and reduce the actual sizes of computers and their related peripherals.

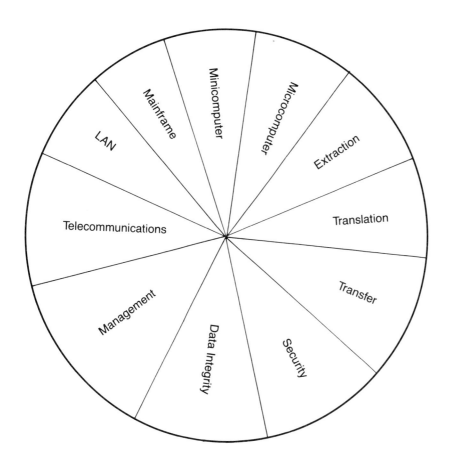

FIGURE 19–1: *Today's MIS managers are faced with tremendous integration challenges. This illustration shows the dominant integration issues.*

MIS managers in large companies often deal with all computing levels; in a small company, a manager may utilize only one or two levels of computing, such as a minicomputer with connecting microcomputers. The MIS manager not only must determine ways to interconnect computing levels but also must maintain security, efficiency, integrity, and administration across all levels. Furthermore, increasing demands by individuals at lower computing levels, such as microcomputer users, for access to data at higher levels, such as a mainframe, have complicated multilevel integration of computing environments.

For the MIS manager, the journey between mainframe and microcomputers can be difficult. However, with the right hardware and software, proper planning, a system-wide architecture plan, technical expertise, and good management, a company can effectively implement a strategy to provide information efficiently across several computing levels.

MIS groups must concentrate on providing access to information throughout an entire company. The advent of the microcomputer has increased the desire of end users to have access to information stored on MIS central computers. The old concept that MIS owns the data and that end users must go through MIS to get information is diminishing. For the most part, MIS groups are looking for innovative ways to provide end users with access to information while maintaining the security and integrity of the information.

MANAGEMENT IN THE INFORMATION AGE

MIS groups are increasingly pressured into providing innovative means of providing on-line access to information. No longer are end users or managers willing to be satisfied with only printed reports generated by complex MIS systems. MIS groups need to place data on-line for end users to manipulate at will. This end-user support is in addition to the production systems that MIS must still maintain. MIS also will need to provide subsets of critical data for end users to manipulate; subsets are needed to ensure the integrity and security of critical information.

Before MIS groups can provide nontechnical end users with access to mainframe data, several aspects of dealing with mainframes must be simplified. A number of technological innovations in hardware and software have been developed to improve informational access for end users. One of the initial simplifications often can be to improve the end user's interface to mainframe environments. For nontechnical people, mainframe can be extremely difficult to use.

Several techniques have emerged that attempt to break the barrier between mainframe-stored information and the nontechnical end user. One of the more successful interface simplifications has been the use of fourth-generation languages.

Fourth-Generation Languages

The term *fourth-generation language* usually refers to a mainframe software product that has been designed to provide the nontechnical end user with an easier interface to mainframe information. Typically, these fourth-generation languages take the form of database management systems (DBMS), financial modeling, and user-definable report writers.

In the area of the fourth-generation DBMS, products such as FOCUS, IDMS/R, and NOMAD provide relational database software technology. These products often serve as front-end interfaces to more complex mainframe systems. The acceptance of these products is attributed to their ease of use, which is the result of the use of English-like commands instead of cryptic computer commands.

Fourth-generation financial analysis and processing products, such as SAS, IFPS, and EPS, serve to give users the capability to access and manipulate mainframe financial data. These products offer managers in nontechnical areas such advanced capabilities as statistical processing, graphics, simulation analysis, and consolidation. These features and others can provide a manager with effective analysis tools for decision making.

Fourth-generation languages put these capabilities under the control of the end user. It should be kept in mind that these languages often serve as the secondary levels of mainframe applications, which means that they often function as a front-end interface to primary applications, such as payroll or accounting systems. Fourth-generation languages offer value-added analysis to these systems.

For the manager outside of MIS, the use of fourth-generation languages provides greater flexibility in decision making, because such languages offer easy, efficient ways of accessing mainframe data. Furthermore, the manager also has the capability to extract, manipulate, and report mainframe information in a variety of ways. The user's ability to use English-like statements, to have immediate access to mainframe data, and to manipulate and report information in a controlled way has contributed to the success of fourth-generation languages.

These products are beginning to open up the vast amount of data stored in mainframe systems. For the manager in the central MIS group, fourth-generation languages can reduce the application development backlog by allowing end users to generate their own simple reports. This allows MIS to concentrate on the development and maintenance of larger, more complex systems. In addition, because fourth-generation languages operate on the mainframe, the central MIS group can still administrate, control, and secure information used by these languages.

Finally, because fourth-generation products are usually software only, MIS groups don't have to be concerned about making changes to mainframe hardware to accommodate these languages. However, because of an increase in the number of people using the mainframe when fourth-generation languages are installed, capacity management of mainframe disk storage and communication lines must be monitored closely.

ENTER THE MICROCOMPUTER

In addition to fourth-generation languages, the microcomputer brings a long list of additional management challenges. The influx of the microcomputer to the desktops of business professionals has caught many firms by surprise. In some cases, hundreds and even thousands of microcomputers enter a company before any clear plan is developed on how to use and support them, how to train employees, and how to control the implementation of these machines. For management, the microcomputer intrusion can be challenging.

Because the microcomputer often falls into the hands of people who are not computer professionals, the challenge is even more complex. Often non-computer-oriented managers are faced with supporting a department full of microcomputers before they are properly trained. These managers frequently make the mistake of assuming that people can use microcomputers without any formal training or on-going support. Both technical and nontechnical managers must understand the issues surrounding microcomputer management.

UNDERSTANDING THE MICROCOMPUTER'S ROLE

Understanding when and how to use the microcomputer is important. The manager in charge of supporting the use of microcomputers must develop a clear plan to insure effective implementation.

In developing such a plan, a manager who has had prior computer-management experience may make more mistakes than a manager who has no computer background. Most managers who have a computer background got their experience in a mainframe-terminal environment. In that central MIS capacity, management thought processes are centered around control. In the microcomputer environment, however, management should be based on coordination, and leadership should be based on advanced knowledge. Although many MIS techniques can be transferred into the microcomputer management role, the assumption that all techniques apply can be painfully incorrect.

Microcomputer managers must also coordinate with the central MIS department in order to construct long-term plans. Although decentralization is an inevitable process for many companies, coordination across decentralized areas must be maintained. Often MIS mainframe-based groups feel pressured and threatened by the explosion of microcomputers; generally, these fears are unfounded, because the MIS group, along with its mainframes and minicomputers, will still exist in most cases. Many of the applications that operate on a mainframe are simply not suitable for operation at the microcomputer level.

For managers to effectively implement microcomputers, they must understand the capabilities and limitations of the micro in comparison to other alternatives, such as the mainframe. Keeping these differences in mind can help a manager decide whether to place a particular application on a mainframe or microcomputer.

MISCONCEPTIONS ABOUT MICROCOMPUTERS

One of the big problems facing managers is overcoming some microcomputer misconceptions. Some of the more common misconceptions include the following:

- Microcomputers are cheaper than other alternatives.
- Everyone should have a micro.
- You don't need training to use a micro.

These misconceptions can lead to fatal and costly implementations of microcomputers in any company.

Microcomputers are not necessarily cheaper than other alternatives. For an individual person or even a small department, the cost of a few microcomputers is definitely lower than that for a mainframe or minicomputer. Upper management, however, must look at the cost of microcomputers from a broader viewpoint. For instance, the installation of 500 microcomputers at $7,000 each would represent a capital outlay of $3.5 million. The often-forgotten cost of such items as disks, magazines, books, paper, furniture, training, and other items can easily raise the total cost to $5 million. That same amount could purchase two IBM mainframes.

If the 500 microcomputers would be given to 500 people for their dedicated use, upper management should look at the mainframe alternative. They must question whether they are getting the same economies of scale from these 500 people that they would have received from the use of two large mainframes, which could accommodate more people. Often the answer to this question leads away from the microcomputer implementation.

For managers to justify the cost of implementing microcomputers, two major issues must be addressed. First of all, managers must prudently implement microcomputers and keep the per-user cost as low as possible. Second, management must ensure the highest amount of business-related productivity and creativity from microcomputer users.

Several techniques can be employed to help reduce the per-unit cost of microcomputers. For example, managers must be certain not to allow pressure from employees to cause them to chase technology. Just because a vendor announces a new microcomputer with a bundle of new features, that doesn't mean that every microcomputer order from that date should be for the newest micro. In some cases, the use of the top-of-line product may be overkill. Managers should purchase computers and related equipment based on requirements and reasonable future needs.

Another cost-reduction technique is sharing; one microcomputer, properly located, might be shared by several individuals. Because of heavy utilization or geographic locations, however, people sometimes cannot share a micro. In these cases, cost reduction can still be realized through techniques, such as local area networks or multiuser micro systems, that allow people to share such peripherals as printers, plotters, and modems.

A common misconception is that everyone needs a microcomputer. Despite what some people would like to think, this is not always the case. Often the first microcomputers to enter a company land on the desktops of managers. It doesn't take long for a microcomputer to become a status symbol, and then every manager in the company wants one. Usually, these microcomputers get too little or too much use by the manager.

When the microcomputer is used too little by managers, it is often because of fear or time restraints. Many managers are simply too busy to sit and work on a microcomputer. Studies have shown that managers typically spend their time in meetings, on the phone, traveling, and handling human relations problems. If this is true, it isn't hard to figure out why many microcomputers in managers' offices simply collect dust. Normally, after a period of time these machines are transferred to staff or assistant personnel, who will use them much more often.

On the other hand, microcomputers sometimes can be used

too much. When people get microcomputers, they may start working on things that are not related to their jobs. It is not uncommon for business professionals, clerks, and managers to turn into programmers and game players when given a micro. This type of activity, outside the scope of a person's job, can become a serious waste of time.

Another common misconception relates to training. Often the success or failure of a microcomputer implementation depends on management's handling of training. Many managers have read computer advertisements that boast "easy-to-use" or "user-friendly" features. This type of advertising has led many managers down the fatal path of ignoring the need for training when implementing microcomputers.

Although the microcomputer is typically much easier to use than traditional mini or mainframe computers, the need for good training still exists. Even experienced mainframe users who acquire a micro often need additional training. Traditionally, users on mainframes deal with the finished products of programmers and analysts. The end user rarely gets involved with the detailed design, coding, testing, and ultimate implementation. In the mainframe world, the end users normally sit at a terminal and perform simple data entry tasks. As a result, the end user has no idea of what actually must occur to make a system operational on a computer.

In addition, many people who are given microcomputers are completely new to computing, and they bring with them all sorts of preconceived fears. The need for training up front is crucial for these workers; without it, their fears may keep them away from the micro altogether.

As managers begin to install hundreds or thousands of microcomputers, the need to actively, efficiently, and effectively use these tools is crucial. The words *productivity increases* are often used in justifying the purchase of micros. True productivity increases can fall short of potential, however, if proper training is not provided to end users. Simply purchasing a micro and placing it on a person's desk will not automatically guarantee productivity. In many cases this approach accomplishes very little. Managers must be willing to give end users both training and on-going support. In the following example, a group of managers learns of the need for training for micro users.

Case Analysis

At Firm A, a large company, a tremendous number of manual tasks were performed each day. As the load increased, management simply hired more people. A new manager arrived at the company and decided that microcomputers could be used to prevent additional hiring and to increase the productivity of existing staff members. The company then spent in excess of $500,000 for microcomputers for its staff of a hundred people — an expenditure of $5,000 per employee.

The management purchased the machines without informing the staff of its decision. One morning, the staff arrived at work and found microcomputers on each desktop. At a meeting later that day, the managers explained that they had purchased the microcomputers to help increase productivity and to diminish the need to hire additional workers. They informed the staff that the micros were easy to use and that software and manuals were available for use. None of the managers had used micros before, and they based their analysis of ease of use on what they had heard and read. The managers also stated that they looked forward to seeing the progress that staff members would make using the machines. At that point, the meeting was ended and the staff returned to their work areas.

As several staff members began to read the manuals on their desks, they became confused by the maze of unfamiliar terminology. The manuals were filled with terms such as *floppy disks, hard disks, booting the system, formatting a disk,* and so forth. These words made no sense to the staff. In addition, simple things, such as how to turn on the computer, proved to be difficult. These factors and others served to cause frustration among the staff and management.

For several months, the microcomputers rarely got any use whatsoever. Management was stunned by the fact that all the wonderful things that they had heard microcomputers could provide didn't happen in their environment. As a result, management decided to call in a consultant to investigate. The consultant interviewed both management and staff to determine possible problems. In addition, he studied the needs of the staff and management. He quickly identified one of the major problems to be the lack of any formal training for the staff.

The consultant pointed out that besides the initial investment of $500,000, an additional $50,000 ($500 per staff member) was needed for training. It was explained to the management that this additional 10-percent investment would help to yield the benefits initially desired. The managers took the advice of the consultant and began formal training. Within two months the staff had completed a detailed training curriculum.

As the consultant had predicted, after the training the staff immediately began using the micros routinely. Instead of collecting dust, the micros became active participants in the daily activities of the staff. The end result was that an additional 10-percent investment in training made all the difference in the success of micros within this company.

Unfortunately, this lack of understanding of the need for training is common in many companies. Managers must not only understand but believe in the need for training if they are to achieve the maximum productivity from these tools and the people who use them.

SYSTEMS DEVELOPED BY END USERS

Another major concern is how to support systems developed by end users using microcomputers. The issues surrounding these user-developed applications can be complex and are often overlooked. Among the applications developed by end users are such things as financial models created using electronic spreadsheets, databases, custom-written programs (using BASIC, C, FORTRAN, etc.), and word-processing documents.

Often managers are pressured into purchasing several microcomputers. When these machines arrive, they are often given out with no boundaries on their uses and no mechanisms to monitor their overall effectiveness. End users are often free to develop whatever systems they feel necessary to do their work. The first job given the micro is usually to automate an operation currently done manually. The end users then might begin to develop new applications to enhance or improve their job functions.

Managers are often unaware of the development that occurs on these micros, which can be disastrous. The issues surrounding systems or applications developed by end users with microcomputers can be complex, but if they are properly understood and adequately planned for, such development can be effectively coordinated and managed.

Some of the more common problems surrounding applications developed by untrained end users are examined briefly below.

1. End user has limited experience or training in application design or development.

Because microcomputers often find their way into nontechnical, non-computer-oriented areas, the availability of individuals capable of developing proper applications on micros can be limited. As a result, companies often find themselves running poorly developed systems on their microcomputers. Managers have a couple of alternatives to counter this problem. One approach might be to provide all end users with access to training courses. A manager may also choose to bring in a consultant to develop custom applications and then turn them over to end users for their use. Another possible approach could be to take one or two individuals from within the organization and provide them with the training to do application development for the entire area. Whatever approach is used, managers should be certain that whoever begins to develop applications on a micro is adequately trained.

2. End users often will not document the applications they have developed on a microcomputer.

The problem of getting people to document what they have done on a computer has existed since the first computers were introduced. In the mainframe world, MIS managers constantly struggle to get programmers and analysts to document their work. Unfortunately, the problem of lack of documentation has permeated to the microcomputer level. Because documentation is something you do after the fact, end users often simply ignore it.

Management should realize that documentation is not for the benefit of the person developing the application. Developers don't document the application because they feel that they understand how to operate it perfectly (that's because they wrote it). Documentation is an insurance policy for managers and their organization. Proper documentation can give a manager the comfort of knowing that if a key employee is temporarily unavailable or leaves the company, the application running on the computer can be processed by someone else. The seriousness of the lack of documentation is normally not realized until it is too late. Although documentation is an extra step for people to perform, managers should insist that it be carried out by anyone who develops an application.

3. Security of information is often overlooked.

Microcomputers use a storage media known as floppy disks, which range in size from 3 inches to 5¼ inches each. Each can store several hundred thousand characters of information. Because the storage media on a micro is so small and portable and can hold so much information, security can be a problem. Once information is on the disk, removal can be easy.

4. End users don't back up their files regularly.

Making back-up copies of files is important. Almost anyone who has used a computer has lost data as a result of unexpected circumstances. If a back-up file had been made recently, the loss of data would have been minimal. The problem is that a person must somehow get into the habit of making back-ups.

If a manager has decided to implement a number of microcomputers, the backing up of files becomes the responsibility of each end user. Because daily business decisions are based on information generated by computers, the loss of a critical file could be disastrous. Management should constantly emphasize the importance of backing up files. If a manager finds that end users are not backing up files, the manager could assign this responsibility to one person in the organization. If microcomputers are interlinked with other microcomputers through such means as a local area network or departmental processor, the back-up process can be easier. Each of these connection schemes allows a manager to centralize the back-up process. Whatever technique is used, managers must implement steps necessary to ensure proper backing up of information.

5. Management overlooks the need for some type of audit and validity check on applications developed on micros.

Managers must be careful not to allow micros to proliferate without some type of control. An often-overlooked technique is the use of audit and validity checks, which are particularly useful when end users are allowed to develop their own applications.

Because daily decisions are made using data from microcomputers, the information base must be accurate. Electronic spreadsheets are often the primary source of inaccurate reporting, because spreadsheets use complex formulas that can be easily entered incorrectly. The end user may or may not catch the error. One way to prevent error-prone reporting can be to assign someone to audit the accuracy of micro-based applications. The increased cost of having someone perform these audits should be weighed against the risk of making decisions based on inaccurate information.

Because the overall success of the micro has been based on end users having control over their own computing, an increase in user-developed applications will inevitably occur. The challenge for management is to understand the implications and effectively react with adequate controls and procedures. Some additional traits that are characteristic of a good end-user application-development environment are listed below:

1. Management awareness
2. Documentation
3. Controls/standards
4. Adequate training for end users and management
5. On-going support
6. Audit trails
7. Back-up and recovery procedures
8. Good security

THE ROLE OF THE INFORMATION CENTER

The microcomputer has created two distinctly different user communities, mainframe users and microcomputer users. These two communities of end users are rapidly coming together under the terminology of mainframe-micro integration. One technique that deals with the issues of end-user computing, mainframe-micro integration, training, and many other services is the *information center* (IC) concept.

The IC concept was introduced by IBM in 1976 and has since been revised several times. The overall concept involves training the supporting end users so that they can use computer hardware and software technologies to the fullest extent. In early stages, the IC dealt with issues surrounding mainframe products. Since the introduction of the microcomputer, however, the IC also has worked with this technology.

Normally, a company's IC is staffed by managers, support analysts, and trainers whose specialty is helping nontechnical end users to take advantage of computer technology. For years the technical group ran the computers, and the others who used the computers were known as end users. The problem was getting the two groups to effectively communicate. The IC was created to help close the gap between the end user and the needed computer resources. The individuals who work in an IC typically possess good human relations skills combined with good technical background relating to both hardware and software. For the end user, the IC provides a human interface to assist in problem-solving, application development, training, and support.

The Information Center from the Mainframe Perspective

One of the major roles that an IC can play is to help ease the access to mainframe data. Many ICs have begun to use fourth-generation languages as a means to ease such access. Before an IC can begin using a fourth-generation language, however there must be a clear understanding of sources of data available to the end user.

Four major data sources exist:

1. External information
2. Production data
3. Extracted and summarized data
4. User-generated data

EXTERNAL INFORMATION Normally, external information is data that are not present on the company's in-house computer. Some end users need to access external public databases, such as the Source, Dialog, Nexis, or any of the thousands of other such databases. More and more companies are using these databases as rapid sources of information for internal decision making.

The IC can play a major role in coordinating access to and on-line information searches of these databases. In order to prevent redundancy, the IC can keep a record of all searches performed by end users; thus, if additional end users request the same information, the IC would have it on file already.

The IC may also want to perform all on-line searches of these databases. Because these public databases hold an enormous amount of data, the search must be narrowed down as much as possible. Each time you access a public database you incur charges for the actual telephone call and CPU usage during the search, in addition to a monthly service charge. The total cost of using a public database can often exceed $20 per hour. Obviously, if a company allows hundreds of its end users to access these databases, the cost would be overwhelming. Thus, although the use of external information can be valuable to a company, controlled access to these environments is encouraged. The IC can play a major role in this coordination process.

PRODUCTION DATA Production data are normally those data that are critical to a company's daily operation. Such data are usually generated from major systems, such as payroll, accounts receivable and payable, order entry, and budgeting. It is crucial to maintain the security and integrity of this information.

Most ICs are not directly involved with the daily operation of production systems, although they may attempt to provide access to subsets of this production data for end-user analysis and reporting. It is important, however, that ICs be in close contact with the MIS group that is responsible for production data. Because production systems are normally the life and blood of a company, every means should be exercised to prevent IC activities from disrupting the routine operation of these systems.

EXTRACTED AND SUMMARIZED DATA   Extracted and summarized data are basically subsets of production data; such subsets are sometimes needed by the end user. In many cases, end users need only a small portion of the information in a production system.

For instance, a manager may want to know only the accounts payable for a particular department. From this kind of desire grows the need for selective extraction and summarization, which allows the manager to deal only with relevant data. This is the type of issue that instigated the creation of many ICs. Fourth-generation languages, query and extraction tools, and report writers all play a major role in accomplishing this goal. Extracting, summarizing, and reporting of information from production systems should be managed closely by the IC.

Some of the key roles that the IC can assume in order to insure proper extracting and reporting are listed below:

1. Install necessary software to ease access to mainframe data
2. Stay in close contact with MIS groups responsible for production systems
3. Help schedule end users' extracting and reporting so as to prevent conflict with production processing
4. Coordinate all extracting and reporting
5. Conduct classes for end users on proper extracting and reporting techniques
6. Set up naming conventions for end users to avoid conflict with production file names

USER-GENERATED DATA   The final source data available to the end user is information that has been generated by the end users themselves. For instance, several individuals in a department may need access to a certain portion of production data every Monday. Rather than have each person extract the same data, one end user could be made responsible for the major extraction and the other end users could report from the already extracted data.

In other cases an end user may need to perform various analyses on the same data. The IC itself can be a source of user-generated data by placing important information, such as bulletins and newsletters, on-line for access by end users. These and many other sources serve to generate end-user data. Once again, the IC can play the role of educator and coordinator of user-generated data.

The Information Center from the Microcomputer Perspective

In some instances, the sheer number of micros entering a company has created the need for a centralized support group such as the IC. The IC's role with regard to micros, like its mainframe role, is centered around helping end users help themselves through coordination and education.

Because the microcomputer is a stand-alone tool, the end user assumes much of the responsibility for its operation. A well-planned IC, however, can provide some important services to microcomputer users:

1. Technical support
2. Product evaluation and recommendation
3. Application-development assistance
4. Acquisition guidelines
5. Installation of hardware
6. Written instructions for software installation
7. Central purchasing of supplies (paper, disks, etc.)
8. Help desk — with hotline
9. Coordination of user group meetings
10. Development of supplemental documentation

In addition, some of the services that the IC offers to the mainframe environment are also helpful for micro users:

1. Management feedback
2. Training
3. Effective marketing to end users
4. Newsletters
5. Mainframe-micro integration planning
6. Awareness of end users' equipment purchases
7. Security and data integrity

The blend between supporting mainframe and micro end-user needs through one functional area benefits both the IC, management and the end-users. Furthermore, the combination of the two helps to facilitate integrated planning, reduces redundancy and brings the end-users closer to both their data and available computer resources. The diagram in Figure 19–9 depicts a common organizational layout of an IC supporting both mainframe and micro end-user products. This is by no means the only way to organize an IC group.

Overall the Information Center concept has proven to be a tremendous management and end-user aid for many companies. The concept of the integrated IC is one that companies endorsing both mainframes and micro end-user products should consider.

SUMMARY

It is important to understand the boundaries and roles that the IC can play with regard to the four sources of data. The IC can be instrumental in easing the access to mainframe data and simplifying the reporting and analysis of those data by end users. In most cases, the IC best serves the company as an educator and a coordinator between mainframe data and end users. In addition, the IC can also be valuable as the coordinator of microcomputer support.

20. Capacity Planning

CAPACITY planning is the process of managing and planning for increased or decreased utilization in computer resources, software, and supplies. In capacity planning, the entire computing environment must be taken into account — storage, telecommunications, processing. A manager can't wait until 2,000 microcomputer users are screaming for mainframe access before starting to plan for telecommunications. By then it's too late; because of typically long procurement processes, most companies will probably not be able to react with sufficient speed if the needs are not anticipated. When those 2,000 users send in their requests for mainframe access, the manager wants to have a new interface already installed so that all that remains is to flip the switch on.

Managers must understand the entire system. People in capacity planning are typically mainframe-oriented; they often think they can just ignore microcomputers. The truth is, however, that those microcomputer users will soon become mainframe users. Today's capacity planning therefore must consider both mainframes and microcomputers.

Many companies have large numbers of employees who have never used a computer. If such an employee needs a computer, he is given a terminal and some difficult-to-use mainframe software. This often encourages him not to use the resource or not to request access in the first place. This situation has changed with the introduction of microcomputers. The microcomputer allows users who have been reluctant to deal with complex mainframe software to join the computing community. The result is often an exponential growth in the user base desiring to connect to the mainframe. This must be taken into consideration in capacity planning.

Capacity planning with regard to the microcomputer has the same considerations as capacity planning with regard to the mainframe. For example, a local area network requires capacity planning; seven more users on the network could mean another hard disk is needed. Even if you're at home and have an Apple computer, you must do a certain amount of capacity planning. If you're near your last disk and you're working, capacity planning tells you that you need more storage, so you go out and buy more disks. A safer procedure would be not to wait until you reach that last disk. When you're halfway through the last box, buy another one.

The same process occurs on the mainframe. If capacity managers anticipate capacity needs, they can synchronize the timing of purchasing with growing needs, so that the equipment arrives when it is needed.

Change-back systems are often thought of as simply a way to bill computer resource use. They can also be useful, however, in capacity planning and in management in general. Charge-back systems can provide utilization statistics so that managers know what's going on — which resources are under-utilized and which are pressing capacity. For example, if one department is using printers much more often than other departments, the manager may decide to relocate a printer. Tracking resource utilization can lead to necessary adjustments in capacity planning.

Mainframe Processing

The actual impact of microcomputers extracting information from the mainframe in varying amounts could possibly have an impact on the processing throughput of the mainframe. Mainframes, by their nature, have been engineered to provide high-speed multitasking operations. This means that several tasks, or jobs, are processed at the mainframe simultaneously.

The mainframe can operate in either a batch or interactive mode. Interactive processing, which is usually more user-intensive, will typically drain more of the mainframe's resources than batch processing. Batch processing is needed to allow large amounts of data to be manipulated at nonpeak processing times. For the most part, batch processing is not user-intensive — the user interacts very little with the overall process. Mainframe-micro products, which are highly interactive, can cause a tremendous resource problem. In selecting a mainframe-micro product, the user must look for one that offers a combination of interactive and batch processing.

The next area to be considered in reference to mainframe processing is performance prediction, which involves the ability to monitor the utilization of various CPU resources at the mainframe. Most mainframe products offer performance-monitoring software that will automatically track the number of users, the number of applications being processed, and the overall efficiency level of the mainframe. With the advent of the microcomputer and the increased number of users, the performance-monitoring software at the mainframe becomes increasingly important. The utilization of the statistics offered by these packages in many cases offers a guideline to the systems engineer as to what additional resources may be needed at the mainframe. These resources could take into account such things as additional CPUs or memory chips.

Furthermore, these performance-monitoring software packages also provide a good indication of processing cycles. They monitor the failure rates of various devices throughout the mainframe. The failure rates will cross all avenues of the mainframe, including such things as the utilization of diskpack, telecommunications interface, and processing. These indicators are usually supplied on written reports that are generated periodically by the performance-monitoring software. Using the software as a capacity management tool or guideline will assist many organizations in planning for additional resources.

Telecommunications

The microcomputer has brought computing to many individuals who were not using terminals or any other computing resource previously. In some cases these users did not have terminals because they viewed the terminal as being too difficult to use. In other cases, users felt that the mainframe software that was available did not address their needs. The advent of the microcomputer has changed such negative reactions to computing. In most cases, new users of microcomputers will eventually want access to the mainframe. As users realize the power and the ease of use of the micro, they begin to see ways to manipulate data that they currently receive as written reports from the mainframe.

In some implementations of microcomputers in large companies, the telecommunications usage has increased more than 30 percent over the past 5 years. It is important to know that the use of microcomputers in companies will not necessarily mean a trend away from the mainframe. In fact, the opposite is often the case.

Increasing the amount of telecommunications service to a mainframe system is not a trivial matter. If an organization is faced with the task of adding new telephone lines to the mainframe, for instance, the time required to get an additional line from the telephone company can be anywhere from one to five months. Obviously, advanced planning of such a requirement is extremely important.

Other telecommunications and acquisition costs must also be anticipated. For instance, the request for additional telecommunications front-end equipment — controllers, protocol converters, or whatever — must go through a certain procurement process. Procurement in most large companies is not a swift process. A delay of five to six months in getting additional hardware can cause dissatisfaction among users and may also result in lower productivity.

In the more traditional environment, standard terminals were easy to monitor and utilize to predict computing resource demands. Terminals were typically approved and purchased through the DP department. The DP department always knew how many terminals were in use and could anticipate their requirements.

In the new micro era, on the other hand, several hundred microcomputers with modems attached can be brought into a company, along with several hundred users who may all need access to the mainframe, without the DP department even being aware of the micros' presence. At that point, the DP department can only react to, not anticipate, the needs of the new users; this situation causes delays in user support and performance degradation of the network. The best way to avoid the problem is for the DP department to be aware of the number of microcomputers being purchased; thus, office automation and information centers must communicate with MIS groups that control mainframe systems and communications.

Mainframe Direct-access Storage

Data on a mainframe can be stored using tape and disk storage or using a direct-access storage device (DASD).

In planning for an increased usage of mainframe storage, some of the same things mentioned for telecommunications apply. Because of the more sophisticated software packages that are becoming available, micro users have two ways to utilize mainframe disk storage. One is data extraction, a method of taking data from the mainframe. Mainframe extractors pull data from the mainframe databases and then put the data on a subdatabase or a subfile, pending its retrieval by the microcomputer user. In a data-extraction environment, as more files are extracted, more disk space is used for storage of subfiles.

The other storage use — one that should be implemented cautiously — is provided by software packages that offer virtual disk capabilities at the mainframe. Various vendors, including IBM, now offer micro storage at the mainframe in the form of virtual, or simulated, disk storage. As was discussed in chapter 7, such virtual disks appear to the micro and its user as just another micro disk drive.

Each microcomputer user can have from 360KB to several megabytes of disk storage at the mainframe. The justification for using virtual disks is to let micro users have access to the vast resources at the mainframe — in this case, disk storage. At the same time, the virtual disk supposedly can lower the cost of micro workstations. In reality, the virtual-disk system merely shifts the cost from the micro level up to the mainframe. If several hundred microcomputer users are given 10MB or more of storage on the mainframe, a significant increase in mainframe storage capacity may be required. This means that additional diskpacks must be purchased for the mainframe.

Moreover, planners must anticipate that virtual-disk use will grow rapidly. If a user can buy a microcomputer workstation and have a hard disk available at the mainframe, in all probability the option will be exercised. Virtual-disk capability thus has an impact on mainframe storage. It also has a direct impact on the telecommunications network. If the user is given storage at the mainframe, the method of accessing that storage is through telecommunications.

Capacity management of disk storage also has something to do with facilities. Disk-storage packs are usually large, expensive devices. If the organization must rapidly add 20 or 30 disk-packs in a mainframe computer room, it may require an increase in the size of the computer room. The work needed to build or expand a computer room can take considerable time.

The trend is to change the primary purpose of the mainframe from processing to management of storage. Mainframes may eventually serve as managers of data storage, while the actual processing occurs on distributed systems. The capacity planning aspect of the mainframe will change rapidly over the next several years.

Capacity Management at the Micro

Most users aren't aware that capacity management is equally relevant at all computing levels. Storage space on even a micro floppy disk should be monitored, because many software packages haven't been written properly to handle a disk error while processing. For example, if you try to save a file and the disk is full, the operating system displays a "disk full" message. Some software packages can't handle that properly, and you lose your information. Therefore, the capacity of the disk becomes the responsibility of the user.

Capacity management is useful for keeping track of memory requirements. As the computer is used for larger applications, such as databases or spreadsheets, the installed memory may be insufficient.

Monitoring disk usage is another example of micro capacity

management. A company is in the middle of a business activity and runs out of disks — suddenly there is no place to store information. A good capacity management system monitors supplies, including paper, printing ribbons, laser printers, toner, and other media.

The same process applies to hard disks. Capacity management includes keeping track of available storage on the hard disk. When the disk reaches capacity, files can be archived off the hard disk onto floppy disks or tapes. Some of the information may be erased. Eventually, additional or larger hard disks may be needed.

SUMMARY

Capacity planning for microcomputers is much more difficult than it is for more traditional computing systems. Often the driving force behind additional microcomputer resource needs is not management, but the person using the micro. For example, requests to attach a micro to the mainframe often come from the micro user. Good planners must anticipate these requests.

Once the mainframe to micro connection is made, the resource demands will usually far exceed those of a mainframe-to-terminal network.

VENDOR DIRECTORY

Microcomputer Local Area Networks

AST
2121 Alton Ave.
Irvine, CA 92714

Banyan Systems, Inc.
135 Flanders Road
Westborough, MA 01581

Corvus Systems, Inc.
2029 O'Toole Ave.
San Jose, CA 95131

Davong Systems, Inc.
217 Humboldt Court
Sunnyvale, CA 94086

IBM
Entry Systems Division
P.O. Box 2989
Delray Beach, FL 38444

Micom-Interlan, Inc.
155 Swanson Rd.
Boxborough, MA 01719

Nestar Systems, Inc.
2585 East Bayshore Rd.
Palo Alto, CA 94303

Novell, Inc.
1170 North Industrial Park Dr.
Orem, UT 84057

Orchid Technology
47790 Westinghouse Dr.
Fremont, CA 94539

Proteon, Inc.
4 Tech Circle
Natick, MA 01760

3Com Corporation
1390 Shorebird Way
Mountain View, CA 94043

Ungermann-Bass, Inc.
2560 Mission College Blvd.
Santa Clara, CA 95050

Network Operating Systems

Digital Research, Inc.
P.O. Box 579
Pacific Grove, CA 93950

IBM
Entry Systems Division
P.O. Box 2989
Delray Beach, FL 38444

Microsoft Corporation
10700 Northrup Way
Bellevue, WA 98004

Novell, Inc.
1170 North Industrial Park Dr.
Orem, UT 84057

Security

Analytics Communications
Systems
1820 Michael Faraday Dr.
Reston, VA 22090

Boole & Babbage, Inc.
510 Oakmead Parkway
Sunnyvale, CA 94086

Digital Pathways
1060 E. Meadow Circle
Palo Alto, CA 94303

IMM Corporation
100 N. 20th St.
Philadelphia, PA 19133

LeeMAH
729 Filbert St.
San Francisco, CA 94133

Norell Data Systems
3400 Wilshire Blvd.
Los Angeles, CA 90010

Racal Milgo Information Systems
6950 Cypress Rd.
Plantation, FL 33318

Cable and Connectors

Anixter
2375 Zanker Rd.
San Jose, CA 95131

Belden Corp.
P.O. Box 1980
Richmond, IN

Trompeter Electronics, Inc.
8936 Comanche Ave.
Chatsworth, CA 91311

Terminal Emulation

AST Research, Inc.
2121 Alton Ave.
Irvine, CA 92714

CXI
10011 North Foothill Blvd.
Cupertino, CA 95014

Digital Communications
Associates, Inc.
303 Technology Park
Norcross, GA 30092

IBM
Entry Systems Division
P.O. Box 2989
Delray Beach, FL 38444

Forte Data Systems
2205 Fortune Dr.
San Jose, CA 95131

PABX — Phone Systems

American Bell, Inc.
6161 Oak Tree Blvd., 4th Floor
Independence, OH 44131

Anderson Jacobson
521 Charcot Ave.
San Jose, CA 95131

CXC Corporation
2852 Alton Ave.
Irvine, CA 92714

Ericsson, Inc.
7465 Lampson Ave.
Garden Grove, CA 92642

GTE Business Communications
9841 York-Alpha Dr.
Cleveland, OH 44133

Harris Corporation
Digital Telephone Systems
Division
1 Digital Dr.
Novato, CA 94947

Intecom, Inc.
24200 Chagrin Blvd.
Suite 334
Beachwood, OH 44122

ITT Telecom
P.O. Box NCRS
Johnson City, TN 37601

Mitel, Inc.
2625 Butterfield Rd.
Oakbrook, IL 60521

NEC Telephones, Inc.
1875 B Hicks Rd.
Rolling Meadows, IL 60008

Nippon Electric Company (NEC)
8 Old Sod Farm Rd.
Melville, NY 11747

Northern Telecom, Inc.
Business Telephone Systems, Inc.
7777 Exchange St.
Cleveland, OH 44125

Rolm Corporation
2659 Townsgate, Suite 101
West Lake Village, CA 91361

Siemens Communications
Systems, Inc.
Telephone Division
5500 Broken Sound Blvd., N.W.
Boca Raton, FL 33431

Telenova, Inc.
102–B Cooper Court
Los Gatos, CA 95030

United Technologies
Communications Group
32111 Aurora Rd.
Solon, OH 43139

Integrated Mainframe-Micro Software

Execucom Systems Corporation
P.O. Box 9758
Austin, TX 78766

IBM Information Systems
900 King St.
Rye Brook, NY 10573

Information Builders, Inc.
1250 Broadway
New York, NY 10001

Mainframe-Micro Link Software

Applied Data Research, Inc.
Route 206 & Archard Rd. CN–8
Princeton, NJ 08540

Banyan Systems, Inc.
135 Flanders Road
Westborough, MA 01581

Computer Associates
International, Inc.
125 Jericho Turnpike
Jericho, NY 11753

Comshare, Inc.
3001 South State St.
Ann Arbor, MI 48104

Cullinet, Inc.
400 Blue Hill Dr.
Westwood, MA 02090

D&B Computing Services
187 Danbury Rd.
Wilton, CT 06897

Info Center Software
171 Main St.
New Paltz, NY 12561

Informatics General Corporation
21031 Ventura Blvd.
Woodland Hills, CA 91364

Management Science America,
Inc.
3445 Peachtree Rd. N.E.
Atlanta, GA 30326

McCormack & Dodge
Corporation
560 Hillside Ave.
Needham Heights, MA 02194

Micro Tempus, Inc.
4 Farnham Place Bonaventure
P.O. Box 1339
Montreal, Quebec H5A 1H1

On-Line Software International
Fort Lee Executive Park
2 Executive Dr.
Fort Lee, NJ 07024

University Computing Company
UCC Tower
Exchange Park
Dallas, TX 75235

Protocol Converters and Emulators

Amdahl Communications, Inc.
2500 Walnut Ave.
Marina Del Rey, CA 90291

AST Research
2121 Alton Ave.
Irvine, CA 92714

Avatar Technologies, Inc.
99 South St.
Hopkinton, MA 01748

Carroll Touch
2800 Oakmont Dr.
P.O. Box 1309
Round Rock, TX 78680

CXI
10011 North Foothill Blvd.
Cupertino, CA 95014

Digital Communications
Associates, Inc.
303 Technology Park
Norcross, GA 30092

Dynatech Packet Technology,
Inc.
6464 General Green Way
Alexandria, VA 22312

Forte Communications
2205 Fortune Dr.
San Jose, CA 95131

Gateway Communications, Inc.
16782 Redhill Ave.
Irvine, CA 92714

Glasgal Communications, Inc.
207 Washington St.
Northvale, NJ 07647

IBM
Entry Systems Division
P.O. Box 2989
Delray Beach, FL 38444

ICOT Corporation
830 Maude Ave.
Mountain View, CA 94039

Innovative Electronics, Inc.
4714 N.W. 165th St.
Miami, FL 33014

InteCom, Inc.
601 InteCom Dr.
Allen, TX 75002

Intelligent Technologies
International
151 University Ave.
Palo Alto, CA 94301

KMW Systems Corp.
8307 Highway 71 West
Austin, TX 78735

LanCom, Inc.
4754 B North Royal Atlanta Dr.
Tucker, GA 30084

Local Data, Inc.
2771 Toledo St.
Torrance, CA 90503

Memotec Data, Inc.
3320 Holcomb Bridge Rd., Ste.
2060
Norcross, GA 30092

Micom Systems, Inc.
4100 Los Angeles Ave.
Simi Valley, CA 93063

Netlink, Inc.
2920 Highwoods Blvd.
Raleigh, NC 27625

Pathway Design
177 Worcester St.
Wellesley, MA 02181

Perle GSD
600 South Dearborn St., Ste. 507
Chicago, IL 60605

Protocol Computers
6150 Canoga Ave.
Woodland Hills, CA 91367

Renex Corporation
1518 Davis Ford Rd.
Woodbridge, VA 22192

Thomas Engineering Company
2440 Stanwell Dr.
Concord, CA 94520

Verilink Corporation
9 Borregas Ave.
Sunnyvale, CA 94086

GLOSSARY

Access method   The technique for entering a shared communications system. Access methods are designed to prevent collisions that occur when workstations attempt to transmit simultaneously onto a shared cable.

Address   The identifying number of a device that is physically or logically attached to a communications network.

Algorithm   A systematic method used to solve a problem.

Analog   A transmission system based on a continuous ratio. Telephone lines carry analog transmissions.

ANSI   American National Standards Institute. In the data-communications area, ANSI establishes standards for transmission codes and protocols.

Architecture   The combined hardware, software, and communications environment.

ASCII   American National Standard Code for Information Interchange. A character set consisting of 7-bit coded characters (8 bits including parity bit). Also, a type of asynchronous protocol.

Asynchronous transmission   A method of data communication in which information is sent at irregular intervals.

Back-up   A procedure for making a duplicate copy of data to be used in the event that the primary data is lost or destroyed.

Bandwidth   The capacity of a communications system across a particular medium.

224

Baseband   A signal that is placed on a communications medium without change. For example, a baseband signal in a computer system carries the computer's digital signals.

Batch processing   The processing of data that has accumulated over a period of time.

Baud   A common unit of measure for data transmissions. A baud equals approximately one bit per second.

Binary synchronous communications (BSC or bisync)   A character-oriented, half-duplex data-communications protocol developed by IBM in 1964. Currently being replaced by SNA/SDLC.

Bisync   See *Binary synchronous communications.*

Bit   Binary digit. The smallest unit of information used in data processing, represented by 1s and 0s.

Bootstrap loader   An input routine used to initiate computer operations.

Bps   Bits per second.

Bridge   A device used to connect identical communications systems; often includes store-and-forward capabilities. Bridges differ from gateways in that bridges do not perform protocol conversion.

Broadband transmission   An analog circuit that provides high bandwidth.

Broadcast   A simultaneous transmission to multiple receiving devices.

BSC   See *Binary synchronous communications.*

Buffer   A storage medium used for holding data while that data is transferred from one device to another.

Bug   A disfunctional area of the computing system, either hardware or software.

Bus   A series of sockets in a microcomputer that allows special-purpose circuit boards to be added to the system to provide additional functionality. In a communications network, a bus is system in which devices are attached to a shared linear cable.

Byte   A group of 8 bits.

CCITT   International Telegraph and Telephone Consultive Committee. A group that recommends data-communications standards.

Chip   A slang term for microprocessor.

Circuit switching   The temporary connecting of two or more communications channels to permit the exchange of transmissions.

CMS   Conversation-monitoring system.

Coaxial cable   A transmission medium with a central conductor and an outer sleeve- or shield-type conductor. The conductors are separated by a dielectric material.

Communications network   A collection of computers, cables, and communications equipment used to interconnect computing systems.

Contention   An access method in which a workstation may take control of a shared transmission line if no other device is currently transmitting.

Controller   A device that manages transmission between a host computer and terminals.

Coprocessor   A special-purpose microprocessor that works in tandem with the CPU.

Cps   Characters per second.

CPU   Central processing unit. The primary data processor in a computer.

CRC   See *Cyclic redundancy check*.

Crosstalk   A condition in which transmission energy radiates from one transmission line and intermixes with another one nearby, causing interference.

CRT   Cathode ray tube. The display tube used in microcomputers.

CSMA   Carrier sense multiple access. A contention access method in which workstations can sense transmission activity on a cable and wait to transmit until the cable is available.

Cursor   A blinking marker used by applications programs to indicate the position of the next character to be keyed.

Cyclic redundancy check (CRC)   An error-detection technique. A number representing the size of the message is generated and sent with each transmission. When the transmission is received, its size is compared with the number to verify that the size of the transmission has not changed.

Data   Information. In computing, information encoded as binary digits.

Database   An organized compilation of data.

Data integrity   The validity or accuracy of information.

DBA   Database administrator. A person tasked with maintaining a company's database.

DBMS   Database management system. A software program used to store and retrieve data within a database.

DCA   Document Control Architecture, one of the areas defined by SNA. Defines the form and contents of documents that office systems can interchange through an SNA network.

DEC   Digital Equipment Corporation.

Demodulation   The conversion of a signal from analog to digital.

DG   Data General.

DIA   Document Interchange Architecture, one of the areas defined by SNA. Defines the way in which requests and documents can be transferred through an SNA network.

Digital   A transmission system based on discrete states, usually the binary conditions, on and off.

Disk   A removable magnetic medium used for long-term storage of computerized data for microcomputers and some minicomputers.

DISOSS   Distributed Office Support System. An IBM host-based information translation, exchange, and routing system.

Distributed processing   A system in which host computers and intelligent workstations store and manipulate data at multiple locations. The main purpose is to keep the computing function close to the end user.

DOS   Disk operating system. In microcomputer terminology, DOS is usually an abbreviation for MS-DOS (Microsoft's disk operating system) or PC-DOS (IBM's version of MS-DOS).

DP   Data processing. The manipulation of information by a computer.

Dumb terminal   A display workstation that has limited editing capabilities but that is generally incapable of performing data processing functions.

Duplex   A two-way transmission system, synonymous with *full-duplex.*

EBCDIC   Extended Binary-Coded Decimal Interchange Code. An 8-bit character set. EBCDIC is the code generated by most synchronous IBM computers.

Edit   To review and modify data as a refinement process. In computing, to verify data for proper form and content prior to storage.

Electronic mail   A computer-based messaging system. Memos, letters, and documents are transmitted to a central repository, from which they can be accessed by the addressee.

Emulate   Imitate. A system that is properly modified can emulate another system, performing all of the functions of the emulated system.

Encryption   The process of systematically altering data to prevent unauthorized persons from reading and using the data.

End user   A person who uses a computing device to perform a task.

Error   In data communications, an unwanted change in content that occurs during the transmission process.

Error control   The process of monitoring data transmissions to detect and correct errors.

Escape character   A nonprinting character that may be used to signal a device, such as a printer, to anticipate an instruction.

Extraction   A process in which desired data in a database is copied and the copy placed in temporary storage preparatory to delivery through a data communications system.

Fiber optics   An information carrier, or medium. In fiber-optic transmissions, information represented by a light signal is transmitted through a flexible glass fiber.

Field   A category of information.

File   A related set of information stored as a logical unit.

Firmware   A silicon wafer that contains an instruction set or application program. The data in the wafer cannot be modified in normal computer operations.

Footprint   The space that a device displaces on a desk or other work surface.

Full-duplex   A simultaneous two-way transmission of data.

Gateway   A device that uses protocol conversion to connect dissimilar communications systems.

Half-duplex   A sequential two-way transmission of data. In half-duplex, only one device can transmit at a given time.

Handshake   An exchange of control sequences between two devices in preparation for transmission.

Hard disk   Also *fixed disk*. A nonremovable magnetic disk used for long-term storage of computerized data.

HDLC   High Level Data Link Control. A bit-oriented data communications protocol.

Hierarchical database   A database structure that resembles an inverted tree. The database is divided into categories, which, in turn, are divided into subcategories.

Host   A computer that provides the processing function for attached terminals and other devices.

HP   Hewlett-Packard.

IBM   International Business Machines Corporation.

IEEE   Institute of Electrical and Electronics Engineers.

IMS   Information Management System. IBM database management software system that also provides communications monitoring.

Initialize   To ready a device for operation.

Input/output (I/O)   The transfer of data between main storage and peripheral equipment.

Integration   The merging of separate environments. The ability to tie all of the diverse resources of distributed processing into one functional system while maintaining the benefits of a distributed environment.

Intelligent workstation   A workstation that has a built-in processor and that can execute programs.

Interactive   A condition in which an end user has an open channel to a computer system, permitting an immediate request/response interaction.

Interface   A logical point at which two systems can interconnect.

Interrupt   A signal that temporarily stops a process, usually so that another process can be executed.

Kilobyte (KB)   1,024 bytes; in common usage, 1,000 bytes.

LAN   See *Local area network.*

Leased line   A transmission line rented for the exclusive use of one party.

Local area network (LAN)   A high-speed data communications network that is usually restricted to a single building or campus.

Logical unit (LU)   A mainstream component in an IBM network; that is, a mainframe computer.

Mainframe computer   A large, multiprocessor computer. The mainframe is designed to serve many users and perform many functions simultaneously.

Management information systems (MIS)   A group of highly trained computer and communications personnel that supports the computing needs of an organization.

Megabyte (MB)   1,024 times 1,024 bytes. In common usage, one million bytes.

Microcomputer   A small computer designed primarily to serve as a single-user workstation. Most microcomputers have only one microprocessor.

Microprocessor   A complex set of electronic circuitry embedded into a wafer of silicon. The microprocessor takes data and manipulates it using basic mathematical functions.

Minicomputer   A computer that supports multiple users. The minicomputer is equipped with multiple processors and is designed to support simultaneous processing.

Modem   An acronym for *modulate* and *demodulate*. A device that converts between digital and analog signals, permitting computers (digital devices) to transmit across telephone lines (analog systems).

Modem pooling   A system in which modems are shared by many workstations.

Modulation   In data communications, the conversion of a digital signal to an analog signal.

Multiplex   To place two or more signals onto the same transmission channel.

Multitasking   The process of one device executing two or more tasks simultaneously.

Multiuser   A system that allows two or more people to share a single software application or processor simultaneously.

Network   A system of interconnected computing devices that can communicate and share resources.

Networked database   A database structure in which two or more hierarchical databases are interconnected.

Node   Any device — computer, terminal, or peripheral — attached to a communications network.

Off-line   Noninteractive. Processing that is performed in isolation.

On-line   Interactive. Processing that is performed during direct communications between a workstation and a computer.

OSI   Open Systems Interconnection. A model that divides the communications process into seven hierarchical layers. Developed by the International Standards Organization.

PABX   Private automated branch exchange. Term used to describe modern telephone systems within a company or building.

Packet switching   A data communications method in which a message is broken into units called *packets*. These packets can be individually addressed and routed through the communications network.

Parity   An error-detection scheme for data communications. The scheme utilizes a constant state or equal value, which can be verified at the receiving end of the transmission link.

Peripheral   A device that is attached to a computer and controlled by it, for example, a printer, a plotter, a disk drive.

Physical unit (PU)   Used within SNA protocol to define the addresses for printers, plotters, terminals, micros, etc.

PROFS   Professional Office System. An IBM office-automation system that runs on a mainframe computer.

Programmer   A person who is trained to write sets of computer instructions called *programs.*

Protocol conversion   The process of translating between two computer protocols so that two dissimilar systems can communicate.

Query   A means of reporting centrally stored information based on selection criteria.

RAM   Random access memory. The volatile, electronic memory in computers in which data is temporarily stored for manipulation.

Real time   Pertaining to processes that keep pace with an actual occurrence.

Record   A unit of information.

Recovery   The process of reclaiming lost data from back-up sources.

Relational database   A database structure in which data is stored in row-column format.

Resource   Something of limited availability. Computers, peripherals, and applications programs are all examples of resources.

RF   Radio frequency.

RJE   Remote job entry. A system of data communications in which data is processed off-line and transmitted as a batch to another system.

RS-232-C   A standard for connecting computer system components. Most microcomputers are equipped with RS-232-C ports.

SDLC   Synchronous data-link control. A data communications protocol invented by IBM and used within SNA.

SNA   Systems Network Architecture. IBM's overall office information system.

SNI   System network interconnection. A means of interconnecting multiple, independent SNA networks.

Supermicrocomputer   A class of computers between microcomputers and minicomputers. Supermicros perform calculations faster than micros and have limited capability to act as host systems.

Synchronous   A type of data communications protocol that transmits data according to a precisely timed clock pulse.

Telecommunications   The combination of telephone and computer technology for a common communications system.

Time-sharing   A process that allows many individuals to share limited resources. Time-sharing is typically found in mainframe and minicomputer environments, permitting the computing resources of these systems to be shared.

Topology   In networking, the physical layout of a communications system.

Translation   The conversion of text and numbers from one format to another.

TSO   Time-sharing option. Software that permits the sharing of a common computing resource.

Twisted-pair cable   Stranded wire used primarily for telephone and short-range computer transmissions.

User-friendly   A term referring to a hardware or software system that is easy to learn and use.

Virtual disk   An area of storage that is isolated electronically from a large disk and made to emulate a physical disk drive.

VM   Virtual machine. A multiuser system used originally on IBM mainframe computers, now being migrated to smaller computers.

XMODEM   An asynchronous protocol that has error-checking capabilities.

INDEX